Presented To:

_____

From:

_____

Date:

_____

Overcoming Gossip

Overcoming

How satan, the Accuser of the Brethren,
Uses Gossip to Fragment the Body of Christ

Gossip

Mark D. Michael

DESTINY IMAGE® PUBLISHERS, INC.
P.O. Box 310, Shippensburg, PA 17257-0310
"Speaking to the Purposes of God for This Generation and for the Generations to Come."

This book and all other Destiny Image, Revival Press, MercyPlace, Fresh Bread, Destiny Image Fiction, and Treasure House books are available at Christian bookstores and distributors worldwide.

For a U.S. bookstore nearest you, call 1-800-722-6774.
For more information on foreign distributors, call 717-532-3040.
Reach us on the Internet: www.destinyimage.com.

ISBN 13 TP: 978-0-7684-3773-7
ISBN 13 E-book: 978-0-7684-8998-9

For Worldwide Distribution, Printed in the U.S.A.

1 2 3 4 5 6 7 8 9 10 11 / 13 12 11

Contents

Introduction

MOST CHRISTIANS HEAR gossip every day. We hear it on the television, on the radio, while riding along in our cars, when talking with friends and acquaintances, and even at work. Most Christians have heard gossip so much and so often that we have begun to question whether it is normal or natural to gossip. After all, we think, *What's so bad about sharing a little personal information about someone to another person?* I believe that type of thinking is the reason why there are so few books out on this very important subject of gossip and also the reason why the enemy is having a field day using the tongues of the saints. Revelation 12:10 identifies satan as the accuser of the brethren. On the surface, we may not appreciate the need for a book on this subject. We could write about satan as a thief or satan as the one who brings sickness or many other aspects of our enemy's warfare. I have chosen, however, to write to inform the Christian troops about this secret weapon of the enemy, which is identified in Scripture by his title, the accuser of the brethren. This secret weapon of the enemy has caused many casualties in the war between light and darkness. Yes, we have the victory: our enemy is a defeated foe. But so many believers need not suffer on the battlefield while we wait for the final trumpet.

Today, one of the greatest problems the Church faces is the fact that most Christians have not matured enough in their faith walk to know we are in spiritual warfare. It is only through maturity and growth in the faith that we begin to realize that there is a battle to be fought. When people are first saved, they are overjoyed with the new life they find in Christ. *Born again* means to them new music, new relationships, new agendas, and many other novelties. As the fledgling saints continue to grow, they are overwhelmed with the joys of salvation. It takes them a while to realize that God has not delivered them into a spiritual oasis where they just blow whistles and sing praise songs the rest of their lives. They soon begin to realize that, although they have been born again, things still go wrong, and there are negative forces in the atmosphere militating against their lives. Their growth in the Word of God brings them to the staunch reality that they are not in an oasis, but in warfare. Apprised of this, they begin to mature faster. They then begin to quote salvation Scriptures like John 3:16 a little less and begin to embrace warfare Scriptures like Isaiah 54:17 a little more. They have come into the reality that they are in warfare, that they have an enemy, and that they must fight to spiritually and physically survive.

What are the evidences of this war? Many Christians sit leisurely on their porches laughing about life and gossiping about each other while our enemy takes advantage. Satan loves it when Christians are immature in the faith and indifferent toward his schemes. When satan finds these types of saints, he does not attack them directly, lest they find out they too are in a spiritual war. He simply lulls them to sleep. He makes them feel that he does not exist and that all this talk about spiritual warfare is just the Church's effort to keep the saints afraid. However, satan is still busy stealthily destroying them while they march prayerlessly on to their doom.

What are the evidences that satan is destroying them? One woman's daughter walks out of the house and is run over by a drunken driver. Another man's son comes down with a crippling disease in the prime of his life. Another woman is almost about to lose her mind. The majority of the Church struggles to pay even the essential bills. There is chaos in our political system. Our school systems are at their lowest ebb ever, and students are disinterested in learning. Ministers are in a state of passive tolerance, preaching feel-good sermons. While all this is going on, the saints sink to the bottom of a satanic abyss, gossiping about and slandering one another. The Church is casually and passively oblivious to the warfare, although we are experiencing the destructive effects of the battle all around us.

My purpose in writing this book is not to deal with the entire battle. There are many books out on the subject of spiritual warfare. What God has called me to do is to apprize you of one aspect of the warfare and one of the secret weapons of the enemy. The purpose of this book is to give you a better understanding of the schemes of the enemy. It is written to expose how satan keeps the saints divided through gossip and evil reporting. Through gossip, he prevents them from effectively engaging him and maintaining an offensive against him. I am tired of burying our troops. I am tired of seeing saints who have superior weapons lose ground in a battle they should actually be dominating.

The Scriptures declare, *"...greater is He that is in you, than he that is in the world"* (1 John 4:4). The Scriptures also declare:

> *(For the weapons of our warfare are not carnal but mighty through God to the pulling down of strong holds;) casting down imaginations and every high thing that exalteth itself against the knowledge of God, and bringing into captivity every thought to the obedience of Christ* (2 Corinthians 10:4-5).

Lastly, the Scriptures declare:

> *For the word of God is quick, and powerful, and sharper than any twoedged sword, piercing even to the dividing asunder of soul and spirit, joints and marrow, and is a discerner of the thoughts and intents of the heart* (Hebrews 4:12).

These three Scriptures indicate that we have superior weapons. The only way we can lose a battle with superior weapons is if we do not prepare to fight. We already have superior weapons; the following pages are written to help us prepare to fight!

Chapter 1
Who Is the Accuser of the Brethren?

Whosoever gossips to you will gossip about you.
—SPANISH PROVERB

NOT MANY YEARS ago, God gave me a revelation about the spirit realm. He began to show me how everything in the spirit realm works on legal grounds. There is a heavenly judicial system that oversees and governs all earthly operations. If people do not understand this, they may obliviously have their blessings hindered by a "legal" infraction. These people may then assume that God is forbearing to bless them, when actually there is a legal impediment pending against them in the heavenlies—a lien against their blessings, if you will. In this legal system, the saints are the ones on trial. God the Father is judge over the universal judicial system, and Jesus is our defense attorney.

We will talk about Jesus' work as defense attorney later. For now, I want us to meet the prosecuting attorney. His primary and most familiar name is satan. Satan has many names, and we will use several of those names in this book to highlight the variations in his destructive work. We may know him as "the devil," "the evil one," "the enemy," or maybe even "lucifer," but we must learn to know him as "the accuser." Revelation 12:10 says:

> And I heard a loud voice saying in heaven, "Now is come salvation, and strength, and the kingdom of our God, and the power of His Christ: for **the accuser of our brethren** is cast down, which accused them before God day and night."

This eschatological Scripture is a prophecy indicating that the Kingdom of God that we await shall surely come to pass. However, this Scripture gives us much more than just the assurance that our Lord Jesus shall prevail. This Scripture also informs us of many other truths. The first is the reality that, until the Kingdom of our Lord is ushered in, our enemy has access to Heaven and is able to stand before God. The second truth we may glean from this Scripture is that the reason satan is before the throne of God is to accuse the brethren.

Who are the brethren? This reference to brethren, as it always does throughout Scripture, refers to the children of God. That means us. At the throne of God *today,* satan is standing before God accusing us of many things. This Scripture also informs us that, until he is cast out at the end of the age, he carries on this work assiduously or, as the Scripture says, *"day and night."* Satan never stops telling God about us, our faults, our sins, and our weaknesses, demanding that our blessings be hindered because of our disobedience.

Many saints have yet to come to know satan as the accuser. Therefore, I want to begin by highlighting some of the scriptural references to satan's work as the accuser. A clear picture of satan as an accuser will help us understand better how he works in our lives, bringing accusation upon us through gossip and evil reporting. Let us consider Jude 1:9, which says,

> *Yet Michael the archangel, when contending with the devil he disputed about the body of Moses, durst not bring against him a railing accusation, but said, "The Lord rebuke thee."*

This is quite an unusual Scripture. God gives us here a bird's-eye view into a dispute between our enemy, satan, and Michael the archangel. The dispute between them is over the body of Moses. We know that, according to Scripture, Moses died in the wilderness (see Deut. 34:1-5), and scholars today say that no one knows the whereabouts of the body of Moses. Here we see that Michael and satan are in a big fuss over the body of Moses. Notice that the text says that Michael *"durst not bring against him a railing accusation."* The word *railing* here means "word for word," or to argue back and forth. Obviously, from an observation of this text, we can see that satan was "accusing" Michael of something, but Michael refused to return his calumnious accusations, saying instead, *"The Lord rebuke thee."* Michael knew satan as an accuser and decided that it would not be God's will for him to join satan in an accusation party.

Let us look now at yet another reference to accusation in the Scripture. Second Peter 2:10-12 says,

> *But chiefly them that walk after the flesh in the lust of uncleanness, and despise government. Presumptuous are*

they, self-willed, they are not afraid to speak evil of dig-nities. Whereas angels, which are greater in power and might, bring not railing accusation against them before the Lord. But these, as natural brute beasts, made to be taken and destroyed, speak evil of the things that they understand not; and shall utterly perish in their own corruption (2 Peter 2:10-12).

In the above reference, we can see clearly that accusation is definitely a part of the spirit realm. In this scriptural reference, the apostle Peter is writing to address the false prophets of his day. His description of them is quite explicit. They walk in their own lust. They are presumptuous and self-willed. By this description we understand that these are carnal-minded people, enemies to the cross of Jesus Christ. But let us look closely at this Scripture because it also references the angels and their relationship to these false prophets. In verse 10 we learn that these false prophets are *"not afraid to speak evil of dignities."* The word *dignities* here refers to the angels of God and the unknown things of God. These false prophets were making statements about angels and claiming to have special insight about God that they did not possess.

Peter brings scathing denunciation upon them, saying they will perish for their arrogance. Notice that verse 11 says that the angels of God would not bring an accusation against these false prophets before God. Verse 12, however, goes on to tell us that these false prophets took great pride in bringing accusation against the angels. This reference to the activity of false prophets allows us to see clearly that they are backed by the accuser. The response of the angels in this text would also give us insight into how God would have us respond to accusation. Just as the angels refused to receive their calumnious words, so should we refrain from receiving accusations against angels and other people.

Now let us get back to our focus on the legality of the spirit realm. There is another Scripture in First Peter that highlights the legality of the spirit realm. Consider First Peter 3:7:

> *Likewise, ye husbands, dwell with* [your wives] *according to knowledge, giving honor unto the wife, as unto the weaker vessel, and as being heirs together of the grace of life; that your prayers be not hindered.*

Sometimes we read Scripture too casually, assuming it is easily understood. When we do, we fail to hear the weighty revelations within the Scripture. The above Scripture admonishes the husband to be knowledgeable of and respectful toward his wife. The reason for this is that, if he does not, their prayers could be hindered. But think about it, God answers prayer. The way many people often interpret this Scripture is to assume that if God sees the disunion or disharmony between a husband and a wife, He would decide not to hear their prayers.

However, let us give sufficient thought to the text. Peter is admonishing husbands and wives how to treat each other, and right in the midst of his instruction, he throws in the phrase *"that your prayers be not hindered."* This is a reference to a third party interfering in the marriage, but this third party is not God. God is informing those of us who are married, through this Scripture, that satan is an accuser and that he will be empowered to attack the marriage and hinder the prayers of the union through disunity if he is allowed. Furthermore, he stands before God blaming us for not being the spouses we should be and, therefore, seeks to hinder our blessings.

This spiritual battleground is spelled out even more clearly in the Book of Daniel. In Daniel 10, Daniel is on a 21-day fast, seeking the Lord for a certain answer to prayer. The Bible says that after 21 days he got a breakthrough visit from an angel who informed him that his prayers had been heard from the very first day he prayed, but hindered. It reads:

> *And behold, a hand touched me, which set me upon my knees and upon the palms of my hands. And he said to me, "O Daniel, a man greatly beloved, understand the words that I speak unto thee, and stand upright: for unto thee am I now sent." And when he had spoken this word unto me I stood trembling. Then said he unto me, "Fear not, Daniel: for from the first day that thou didst set thine heart to understand, and to chasten thyself before God, thy words were heard, and I am come for thy words. But the prince of the kingdom of Persia withstood me one and twenty days: but lo, Michael, one of the chief princes, came to help me; and I remained there with the kings of Persia"* (Daniel 10:10-13).

Here again we can easily see that there is a correlation between the natural realm and the spirit realm. Daniel's fasting and prayers were affecting Heaven. The angels were responding by carrying messages from God and revelations in the spirit realm. But none of this was done without satanic opposition and interference. God desired to bless Daniel, but satan was looking for a way to hinder Daniel from being blessed.

Now let's add a hypothetical element to this situation. Let's say Daniel had some sin in his life. The accuser of the brethren would have hindered this breakthrough even longer because he would have swiftly come before God and declared, "Daniel is unworthy to receive the revelation he was waiting for!" This is satan's job as prosecuting attorney and accuser of the brethren. He is before God daily to influence Heaven from granting our request and desires.

Because we are not perfect and do make mistakes from time to time, God has provided for us a defense attorney. Don't panic; we don't even have to pay this attorney. His services are all "pre-paid legal" services. God paid for our defense attorney by the blood of Jesus over 2,000 years ago. Whenever the accuser stands to blame us, Jesus as our defense attorney comes to our defense. What a joy we have in Jesus. Before we look at Jesus as defense attorney, I want to look at a few more instances of satan as the accuser of the brethren and prosecuting attorney.

In the Book of Job, we find an interesting corroboration for all I have stated thus far. Job was God's man; he was *"...perfect and upright, and one that feared God and eschewed evil"* (Job 1:8). Job had seven sons and three daughters and was very wealthy. While all was peaceful on the home front, there was a judicial battle going on in Heaven over Job and his blessings. The accuser of the brethren was standing before God, appealing to God against Job and accusing Job. Don't just take my word for it; let's look at the courtroom clerk's journal:

Now there was a day when the sons of God came to present themselves before the Lord, and satan came also among them. And the Lord said unto satan, "Whence comest thou?" Then satan answered the Lord and said, "From going to and fro in the earth, and from walking up and down in it." And the Lord said unto satan, "Hast thou considered My servant Job, that there is none like him in the earth, a perfect and a upright man, one that feareth God and escheweth evil?" Then satan answered the Lord, and said, "Doth Job fear God for naught? Hast not Thou made a hedge about him, and about his house, and about all that he hath on every side? Thou hast blessed the work of his hands, and his substance is increased in the land. But put forth Thine hand now and touch all that he hath and he will curse Thee to Thy face." And the Lord said unto satan, "Behold, all that he hath is in thy power; only upon himself put not forth thine hand." So satan went forth from the presence of the Lord (Job 1:6-12).

Of course there are many points to this story, but the primary point I am stressing here is that, despite Job's righteous life, the accuser was still at work seeking to destroy him and all that he had. Because satan had no direct accusation against Job, he resorted to saying that Job was only serving God for the fringe benefits of it, that Job really did not love God. God decided to amuse the accuser so that we could benefit from Job's testimony. There is much to be learned here. First and foremost, we should realize that if satan has the sense enough to stand before God's throne and accuse us, we ought to be spiritually astute enough to understand the importance of our own prayers to God. Every spiritual battle is won or lost before the presence of God. What is happening on earth to us in a negative way today is a manifest token of lost battles in Heaven. It is as simple as this: If satan is up there talking to God about us, we should be in our prayer closets talking to our attorney about our situations.

After satan left the presence of God, he smote Job with sickness, disease, and destruction. All his family, sheep, and property died or were destroyed. The only thing Job had left was a nagging wife. I wonder why satan did not take her? Nevertheless, we can also see that some natural catastrophe is a direct result of the work of satan. Often when a hurricane or tornado or terrible car accident takes a loved one, we spend years blaming God for it when the culprit was really satan. We would do well to take note of how committed the enemy is to destroying us. We should begin to take prayer and the study of God's Word more seriously.

The final place I would like to look at satan as accuser is the eighth chapter of the Book of Romans. Paul is writing to the church at Rome, and in the eighth chapter he asks a series of questions, all of which have implied answers. If we understand Paul's implications, we can easily see that Paul had been given a revelation of satan as the accuser. I have inserted the answers to pertinent questions in brackets within the text, so that we can more easily see the significance of Paul's revelation. He writes in Romans 8:31-35:

> *What shall we then say to these things? If God be for us, who can be against us?* [satan] *He who spared not His own Son but delivered Him up for us all, how shall He not with Him also freely give us all things?* [by grace] *Who shall lay anything to the charge of God's elect?* [the accuser] *It is God that justifieth: who is he that condemneth?* [satan, the prosecuting attorney] *It is Christ that died, yea rather, that is risen again, who is even at the right hand of God, who also maketh intercession for us.* [Jesus, our defense attorney] *Who shall separate us*

from the love of Christ? [satan will try in the following ways] *Shall tribulation, or distress, or persecution, or
famine, or nakedness, or peril, or sword?*

Once we understand satan as the accuser, we can easily see the
significance of Paul's argument. He is making a case for the saints
who are being accused in Heaven. He argues first in Romans 8:30
that we have already been called, justified, and glorified. Thus, he
claims spiritual impunity of our eternal state from the attack of
the devil. Paul knows satan cannot touch our position in Christ.
That is forever settled. Satan can, however, cause havoc for us in
this life with tribulation, distress, famine, and many other things.
Paul argues against the accuser, stating that Christ has died for us
and is even now defending us before God.

Praise God for our defense attorney! He is constantly standing
before God on our behalf, pleading the atoning blood over our
every sin and weakness. If we did not have an attorney in Heaven,
even though we are saved by Jesus' blood, our lives would be as
miserable as Job's life was in his unprotected and undefended
state. We would remain under the constant attack of satan. Paul
had been given a revelation of satan's work of blaming us before
the Father. He wrote the eighth chapter of Romans to establish us
in the truth that, though we have to play legal chess in securing
our blessing sometimes, we know that in the end nothing shall
separate us from the love of Christ.

The Adjudication

In Heaven, the court scene is likened to a courtroom here
on earth. The accuser may come before our heavenly Father and
say, "One of Your daughters is a liar. I have a record of her lying

tongue. I request the right to cause her to lose her job." Then the defense attorney, Jesus, rises up and says, "Father, she is also a worshipper. She praises Me daily. I plead immunity on her behalf because of My blood." The Father then says, "Immunity granted on account of the blood." Then the enemy says, "She committed adultery a while back. She must be punished! I request the right to expose it and destroy the marriage." Jesus then steps up and says, "She confessed that sin and asked for forgiveness. I have both forgiven her and cleansed her, Father." Then the Father says, "She is forgiven, accuser. It is forever forgotten; do not bring that matter up again!"

This legal process is ongoing, not because the sin debt is not paid, for Jesus purchased salvation for us once and for all on the cross. He is not defending us so that we can go to Heaven when we die, for salvation is sure. Jesus is defending us so that we can live in peace down here on earth despite the fact that we sometimes miss the mark and sin.

Intercession

Because of this judicial battle that is always waging in Heaven, God has implemented the ministry of intercession. Through intercession, we are empowered through prayer to participate in the heavenly court system. The deliverance from Egypt is one of the most prominent biblical "types" for redemption in the Old Testament. The Israelites were redeemed from their Egyptian bondsmen by the blood of the lamb (see Exod. 12). The wilderness walk then becomes a type of the Christian walk and experience after redemption. The Israelites had been redeemed from Egypt, but they did not yet know the ways of God.

This is how we are when we are first saved. The salvation experience is wonderful, but it does not teach us all that we need to know about God. We must learn to walk with Him in wilderness experience if we are to ever reach the maturity of living in the Promised Land. One of the most prominent wilderness lessons is the lesson of intercession. Moses and Aaron are two people who show us "in type" the ministries of our Lord Jesus Christ. Moses was an intercessor and fulfilled "in type" the present day ministry of Jesus Christ as our intercessor (see Heb. 7:25). Aaron was a high priest and fulfilled "in type" the present day ministry of Jesus as our great high priest (see Heb. 4:14-15).

Most Christians are inclined to think that, if they are born again, they do not need an intercessor or a high priest, but the opposite is true. Although Israel had been redeemed and had become the people of God, because they had to stand before God's holiness in their imperfect state, they needed an advocate to plead their case. They were redeemed, but imperfect people who struggled to grow into the full will of God. We shall one day receive our new resurrection bodies and be delivered from the presence of sin, and then we will no longer need an advocate. Today, we praise God for Jesus and His role as our advocate (defense attorney) and our high priest.

In the Old Testament, we see Moses in his intercessory prayer ministry in the wilderness of Sin. The people began to murmur against Moses because they would not accept the walk of faith. We read in Numbers:

And all the children of Israel murmured against Moses and against Aaron: and the whole congregation said unto them, "Would God that we had died in the land of Egypt! Or would God we had died in the wilderness. And wherefore hath the Lord brought us unto this land, to fall by the sword, that our wives and our children should be a prey..." But all the congregation bade stone them with stones... (Numbers 14:2-3,10).

This attitude angered the Lord, and His wrath was turned against them. But thanks be to God, Moses fulfilled his role as their intercessor. Numbers 14:5 says, *"Then Moses and Aaron fell on their faces before all the...congregation...of Israel."* There Moses and Aaron remained in prayer until God spoke:

And the Lord spoke to Moses saying, "How long will this people provoke Me? And how long it be ere they believe Me, for all the signs which I have showed among them? I will smite them with the pestilence, and disinherit them, and will make of thee a greater nation and mightier than they" (Numbers 14:11-12).

Moses, however, was a good intercessor and did not allow his own desire to be blessed to prevent him from praying for the people. His words back then are the words that Jesus Christ is praying for us today in Heaven even when we sin and fail. Moses prayed:

Pardon, I beseech Thee, the iniquity of this people according unto the greatness of Thy mercy, and as Thou hast forgiven this people from Egypt until now (Numbers 14:19).

The response of the Lord to the intercessory prayer of Moses is also the same as His response to the intercessory prayer of our

Lord Jesus Christ as He prays for us today. In Numbers 14:20 the Lord says to Moses, *"I have pardoned according to thy word."* Hallelujah.

Jesus Our Intercessor

Who is he that condemneth? It is Christ who died, yea rather, that is risen again, who is even at the right hand of God, who also maketh intercession for us (Romans 8:34).

If the Lord would forgive the transgressions of Israel under the Old Covenant, we know that today we have a better covenant predicated upon better promises (see Heb. 8:6). We also have a far better intercessor than Moses in the Lord Jesus Christ. If God's response to Moses' intercessory prayer was an unequivocal, *"I have pardoned according to thy word"* (Num. 14:20), how much more shall God not pardon according to the intercessory prayer of His Son Jesus. We are already aware that there is one who condemns us before God—the accuser, satan. Even when we have blown it and done the unthinkable, we have recourse in Jesus.

First John 2:1 reads, *"My little children, these things write I unto you that you sin not. And if any man sin we have an advocate with the Father, Jesus Christ the righteous."* Romans 8:34 also says that Christ died for us, rose from the dead, and is now at the right hand of God making intercession for us. Jesus is praying for us, and His prayers are effective with God. If satan failed to have Israel condemned back in the wilderness, how will he have victory over us who have the Holy Spirit living within us and Jesus as our intercessor and high priest?

The Holy Spirit Our Intercessor

For this same reason, we have been given the Holy Spirit. One of the works of the Holy Spirit is to convict the world of sin (see John 16:8). However, He has another work, which is that of making intercession for the saints. Romans 8:26 says:

Likewise the Spirit also helpeth our infirmities: for we know not what we should pray for as we ought: but the Spirit itself maketh intercession for us with groanings which cannot be uttered.

This Scripture is apprising us of the intercessory work of the Holy Spirit. The Holy Spirit is in the courtroom of Heaven as a witness and a second attorney on our behalf. Here on earth, the Holy Spirit helps our "infirmities" or our weaknesses, in that we do not know how to pray to God our heavenly Father as we should. In Heaven, the Holy Spirit acts as a witness on our behalf. He is called to the stand to testify of our growth and development as believers. Satan stands to accuse us before God. Jesus, our intercessor, acts as our defense attorney. But we participate in this judicial system through our personal prayers, which are guided by the Holy Spirit.

As we stand in prayer, asking God for forgiveness for any sins we have committed, as we pray for others, and as we agree with the Word of God in prayer, we make our defense sure. The Holy Spirit's work is to guide us onto the witness stands of Heaven through prayer to make a good deposition before God. In this way, He helps us to overcome our weaknesses and makes us able to testify before God that we stand blameless. Thank God for the work of the Holy Spirit and thank God for Jesus our intercessor and advocate.

The term *advocate* is a legal term that connotes someone who defends someone else, such as a lawyer or defense attorney. Consider again First John 2:1, *"My little children, these things write I unto you, that ye sin not. And if any man sin, we have an advocate with the Father, Jesus Christ the righteous."* The tone of this Scripture is quite legal. We can easily extrapolate that the holiness of God is constrained each time we sin. Because of this, satan can demand that our sins be punished or that we lose our natural blessings. For this reason, John declares that the ideal situation for Christians is that we live holy lives. This is the will of God, that we abstain from all forms of sin.

However, John acknowledges that the probability of the saints sinning is high, therefore he says, *"If any man [does] sin, [he has a lawyer]."* Even though some of us have been far from perfect, we have a lawyer and an advocate in Heaven. We need not sob and cry over our failures. Instead, we tell our attorney through prayer and seek forgiveness. Our lawyer is Jesus Christ—the righteous one. When we had no righteousness, God gave us righteousness through His Son Jesus. He is our attorney, and He has never lost a case. He knows the judge personally. We can have forgiveness today if we would repent and pray.

Jesus Our High Priest

And he shewed me Joshua the high priest standing before the angel of the Lord, and satan standing at his right hand to resist him. And the Lord said unto satan, "The Lord rebuke thee, O satan; Even the Lord that hath chosen Jerusalem rebuke thee: Is not this a brand plucked out of the fire?" Now Joshua was clothed with filthy garments, and stood before the angel. And He answered and spake unto those that stood before Him saying, "Take away the filthy garments from him." And unto him He said, "Behold, I have caused thine iniquity to pass from thee, and I will clothe thee with change of raiment." And I said, "Let them set a fair mitre upon his head," so they set a fair mitre upon his head, and clothed him with garments. And the angel of the Lord stood by (Zechariah 3:1-5).

The third chapter of the Book of Zechariah contains a very interesting revelation about the importance of the high priestly office and the role of satan as the accuser. The scene can be applied to the heavenly reality of Jesus as our high priest or to an earthly reality of a human high priest. We will look at it here from the perspective of an earthly high priest. In either case, however, the work of the accuser is the same. There are certain key verses that are important to understanding what is actually going on.

Zechariah 3:1 says, *"And he shewed me Joshua the high priest standing before the angel of the Lord, and satan standing at his right hand to resist him."* The word resist here can be interpreted *"accuse."* The principle here is that, if God accepts the high priest, He is accepting all of Israel. If God rejects the high priest, He is rejecting all of Israel. It would greatly please satan for God to reject Joshua. Therefore, the "resisting" referred to here is the work of the enemy accusing Joshua before God.

We might ask the question, "If Joshua is doing the work of God, how can satan resist him?" From a natural perspective, we know that the high priest was to live a holy life before God because he had the responsibility of coming into the presence of

God each year to offer sacrifices for the people. Zechariah 3:3 says, *"Now Joshua was clothed with filthy garments, and stood before the angel."* This statement is a reference to the fact that there was sin in Joshua's life. Satan was knowledgeable of the sin and was standing there to accuse Joshua and to request that God reject both Joshua and Israel. But God's response to satan's accusations was, *"The Lord rebuke thee, O satan; even the Lord that hath chosen Jerusalem rebuke thee. Is not this a brand plucked out of the fire?"* With these words, God was reminding satan that Joshua had been redeemed and that he would not validate his case. We too have been redeemed and God has validated us in Jesus Christ.

Instead of receiving the accuser's testimony against Joshua, God began the work of sanctifying the high priest. Zechariah 3:4 says, *"'...take away the filthy garments from him.' And unto him He said, 'Behold, I have caused thine iniquity to pass from thee, and I will clothe thee with change of raiment.'"* The accuser is ever before God to condemn us, but God has clothed us with His righteousness, and the enemy's accusations will not stand.

> *Seeing then we have a great high priest, that is passed into the heavens, Jesus the Son of God, let us hold fast our profession. For we have not a high priest which cannot be touched with the feeling of our infirmities; but was in all points tempted like as we are yet without sin* (Hebrews 4:14-15).

Jesus is our high priest. In the Old Testament, Aaron was the first high priest. His job was to offer sacrifices to God for the sins of the people. Once a year, the high priest went into the Holy of Holies to offer sacrifices for the sins of all the people. The high priestly ministry was that of a mediator between God and people.

Hebrews 8:6 says that Jesus *"is the mediator of a better covenant."* As our High Priest, Jesus has "once offered" His blood as the propitiation for our sins. He does not need to continue to offer sacrifices yearly. His body and blood have forever satisfied the holiness of God. Yet, He still stands before God as high priest to remind God of the precious blood that He shed and as a witness that we have been made righteous by that blood.

This same high priest is also our intercessor. The Scripture above says that what makes Jesus such an excellent high priest is that He can be touched with the feeling of our infirmities. This word *infirmities* means weaknesses or human frailties. It is the same word used in Romans 8:26 referring to the Holy Spirit's intercession, saying, *"the Spirit also helpeth our infirmities...."* Here we see that the writer of Hebrews is saying that Jesus can be touched with the feeling of our infirmities. That is to say, He knows what it is like to be human and tempted to sin.

It is a comfort for me to know that the one I pray to about my sins is familiar enough with temptation to know that it can sometimes be difficult to overcome. Although Jesus never sinned, the Scriptures declare He was tempted at all points as we (see Heb. 4:15). Praise God for an empathizing advocate. When the accuser stands before the Father to speak ill of us, we have the intercession of the Holy Spirit, a high priest who has made the perfect sacrifice to God, and an intercessor who understands what we are going through. We have all we need for our victory.

Chapter 2

The Accuser on Earth

But the unbelieving Jews stirred up the
Gentiles, and made their minds evil affected
against the brethren (Acts 14:2).

NOW WE KNOW what is going on in the heavenly courts. However, satan is not the accuser just when he is in Heaven. He is also the accuser right down here on earth. In this chapter, I want to look at the accuser's work here on earth. I would begin this section by reminding us of Paul's admonition to the saints not to be ignorant of satan's devices (see 2 Cor. 2:11). A part of our warfare is knowing how the enemy operates. One of the chief aims of the accuser on earth is that of causing division among the saints. The spirit of accusation always brings strife and division, and where there is disunity and division, there is powerlessness.

Since the enemy does not have a physical body, he uses the hands, mouths, and feet of human beings to do his work. When we find the spirit of accusation working in people, it is often the work of satan and his minions. The demonic forces of the enemy are always around us, tempting us to carry out satan's accusatory policies. Once we come to know satan as the accuser, we know that those who are in league with him are those who are acting and speaking in an accusatory manner. Also, once we understand satan as the accuser, we can see him so evidently in the background of Scripture, working diligently to create discord and to hinder the Gospel. Mark 15:3 says, *"And the chief priests accused* [Jesus] *of many things: but He answered nothing."* Where was satan during the trial of Jesus? Was he asleep? No. He was right in the middle of the action, accusing Jesus and trying to have Him crucified. The chief priest were being used by the accuser to have Jesus killed.

In his ministry, the apostle Paul suffered many horrendous and sinister acts by the Jewish leaders as well as others. But they were not acting alone. The accuser himself was behind their activity. In Acts 24, Paul is in prison and he has to stand before the high priest concerning charges against him for preaching the Gospel. Consider Acts 24:1-2:

> *And after five days Ananias the high priest descended with the elders, and with a certain orator named Tertullus, who informed the governor against Paul. And when* [Paul] *was called forth* [from prison], *Tertullus began to accuse him, saying....*

In this text, it is easy to see that Tertullus is an instrument of the accuser. When was the last time you heard a sermon about Tertullus? Where was the accuser during the trials of Paul? He was right in the middle of things using Tertullus' mouth. Where is the accuser in your church, school, business, or social group? Again, he is right in the middle of things, using whoever will lend him a mouth to create discord, division, and every evil work.

Peter's Rebuke

Then Peter took Him, and began to rebuke Him, saying, "Be it far from Thee, Lord: this shall not be unto Thee." But He turned, and said unto Peter, "Get thee behind Me, satan: thou art an offence unto Me: for thou savourest not the things that be of God, but those that be of men" (Matthew 16:22-23).

Peter was an outspoken disciple of Jesus from the very first day Jesus called him. He seemed to like being in charge. One thing Peter did not understand was that satan has the power to suggest thoughts into our minds. Although satan cannot make us act or speak, he can suggest thoughts to us. This is why we must learn to discriminate between the origins of our thoughts. Some thoughts come from our "self." This includes the suggestions of our minds, our flesh, and our subconscious. Some thoughts come from the Holy Spirit, and some thoughts come by way of the suggestion of satan. Therefore, we have the daily task of guarding our minds and scrutinizing our thoughts to prevent satan from using our mouths. Many of us have come to know the destructive power that words unfitly spoken can have. Many have also come to know that words, once spoken, cannot be retracted.

In the above text, Jesus tells His disciples that He must suffer and die on the cross. This was not exactly what the disciples had in mind for Jesus. Therefore, Peter pulled Jesus aside and began to scold Him and tell Him that He would do no such thing as die on a cross. Jesus' response to Peter teaches us much about how the accuser works on Earth. Jesus says to him, *"Get thee behind Me, satan!"* Notice He does not say, "Get thee behind Me, Peter." The reality is that Peter allowed satan to use his mouth by way of suggesting thoughts into his mind. To Jesus, this act directly aligned Peter with satan, so much so, that Jesus could call Peter, satan.

This reality has profound impact on our analysis of saints who give no thought to their speech. When saints inordinately gossip about people, giving no thought to what they say, they become little "satans," running here and there to do his bidding. This is why satan does not want the saints to awaken to the importance of renouncing gossip.

Can I Sin With My Mouth?

Some people believe that we cannot sin with our mouths. Often this is the reason why many saints have not sought to discipline their speaking habits or curtail their negative conversation. However, we can and do sin with our mouths. For confirmation of this truth, I would like to look a portion of Scripture in the Book of Job. Job 2:9-10 says,

> Then said [Job's] *wife unto him, "Dost thou still retain thine integrity? Curse God, and die." But he said unto her, "Thou speaketh as one of the foolish women speaketh. What, shall we receive good at the hand of God, and shall we not receive evil?" In all this **Job did not sin with his lips**.*

Notice that in last phrase, that Job did not *"sin with his lips."* I believe many people on judgment day will have mountains of sins to answer for that will be the result of loose lips. We need to begin to take our conversation more seriously. Jesus said in Matthew 12:36, *"But I say unto you, that every idle word that men shall speak, they shall give account thereof in the day of judgment."* Here on earth we are in a warfare, and our enemy would like to employ our lips just like he employed Job's wife's lips. How did I conclude that it was the enemy who employed Job's wife's lips? Is that speculation? Not at all; listen to what she told Job, *"Dost, thou still retain thine integrity? curse God, and die."* Where did she get that idea? She got it from the accuser.

In the previous chapter, satan is speaking to God and he says, *"But put forth thy hand now and touch all that he hath, and he will **curse thee to thy face**"* (Job 1:11). Job's wife, like Peter, was not speaking for herself; she was speaking for and doing the work of the accuser. Here is a truth—satan has no authority on this earth because he does not have a body (see Heb. 10:5). Therefore, if he wants to cause division among the saints, he needs your lips to sow discord. If he wants someone slandered, he needs your lips. If he wants malicious gossip spread, he needs to employ your lips. We would think that, as the saints, we would not want satan to use us for his means, but he does use many of us daily. It is a shame to say we are on God's team if satan uses our mouths to run his errands on a regular basis.

Uncleanness

In the Old Testament there were certain things that made a person "defiled" or "unclean," like touching a dead corpse or having leprosy (see Lev. 5:2). To be unclean was a very ignominious thing. If people were considered unclean, they were separated from the rest of the nation and quarantined for a certain period of time. To be cleansed from this defilement, people would have to partake in certain ceremonial rituals that usually involved the priest.

Jesus put an end to the practice of calling people unclean for different infractions against the law. Listen, however, to Jesus' words in Matthew 15:11: *"Not that which goeth into the mouth defileth a man; but that which cometh out of the mouth, this defileth a man."* The ministry of Jesus is the foundation of our present day New Testament ministry. Here in Matthew 15:11, Jesus says that people are not defiled by outward things, but are instead defiled by what comes out of their mouths. Not only have we identified gossip as a sin, now we have also identified it as that which "defiles" or makes people "unclean."

James was the brother of Jesus and the pastor of the church at Jerusalem. In his sermon to his congregation, he also writes, *"The tongue is a fire, a world of iniquity: so is the tongue among our members, that it **defileth the whole body** and setteth on fire the course of nature; and is set on fire of hell"* (James 3:6). In the Old Testament, "uncleanness" or being "defiled" constituted a separation from God. Unclean people were forbidden to approach God. In our day, through the disordered use of the tongue, many have become defiled and caused a gulf between themselves and their God. They have broken fellowship through the sinful use of their tongue. The only way true fellowship will be restored between them and God is through confession and repentance.

Gossiping Chaldeans

In Daniel 3 there is a story about three Hebrew boys named Hananiah, Mishael, and Azariah. They are better known as Shadrach, Meshach, and Abednego. The story goes that King

Nebuchadnezzar made a large image of gold and commanded everyone in the province of Babylon to bow down and worship the image when they heard the sound of the band. Whoever did not fall down and worship the image would be cast into a burning fiery furnace. When all the people heard the big band, they all fell down and worshiped the image the king had set up. But even back there in Babylon, the accuser was busy at work doing his usual thing. Again, satan has no physical body on the earth and, therefore, no authority. If he wants to persecute the brethren, he has to have someone do the job for him.

Daniel 3:8 says, *"Wherefore, at that time certain Chaldeans came near and accused the Jews."* Note the use of the word *accused.* These Chaldeans went in to tell King Nebuchadnezzar that, although he had made this great image and commanded that all in the province should bow down and worship it, there were certain Jews (believers in God) in the province who were not bowing down to the image. We know the rest of the story quite well. The king called for Shadrach, Meshach, and Abednego and questioned them. They confessed that they had not bowed down to the image and that they would not bow down to it. King Nebuchadnezzar was infuriated with the Hebrews, and to make a show of his authority, he commanded that the furnace be heated up seven times hotter than was normal. Then he commanded that the three Hebrews be seized and thrown into the burning furnace.

All of this trouble for these men of God was caused by gossiping (accusing) Chaldeans. Yet, God delivered the Hebrews from both the king and the gossips. When the king saw that the fire did not consume the Hebrews, he thought about how all the conflict started. It all started from the Chaldeans' telling him things about

Shadrach, Meshach, and Abednego. When he realized that he had gone through the embarrassment of having his officers killed, and people witness these Hebrews delivered from his furnace by their God he made a declaration. In Daniel 3:29 he says:

> *Therefore, I make a decree, that every people, nation, and language, **which speak anything amiss** against the God of Shadrach, Meshach, and Abednego, shall be cut in pieces* [he decided not to go with the furnace again] *and their houses shall be made a dunghill: because there is no other God that can deliver after this sort.*

Notice the king directed the prohibition against those who would "speak anything against...." He was turning his anger on the town gossips and telling them to mind their own business. We cause much trouble for people when we open our mouths against them. It is important that we as children of God learn to chasten our tongues and consider the harm we are doing to others with our mouths.

Rick Joyner was given by God a prophetic vision of the last end-time battle between the forces of darkness and the children of light. He wrote down his vision in a book entitled *The Final Quest*. It is interesting to note that in Joyner's vision satan is revealed and referred to as "the accuser." I believe God is bringing the Church into a greater understanding of satan as the accuser of the brethren in these last days. This prophetic vision is for the purpose of our understanding the spiritual warfare that we are involved in every day. Understanding this prophetic vision can assist us in understanding how we might combat the enemy. I will only share here a few short excerpts from the vision that are relevant to the subject at hand:

The demonic army was so large that it stretched as far as I could see...The foremost division marched under the banners of Pride, Self-righteousness, Respectability, Selfish Ambition, Unrighteous Judgment, and Jealousy...The primary strategy of this army was to cause division on every possible level of relationship—Churches with each other, congregations with their pastors, husbands with their wives, children with parents, and even children with each other...The most shocking part of this vision was that this horde [of demons] was not riding on horses, but primarily on Christians...These people professed Christian truths in order to appease their consciences, but they lived their lives in agreement with the powers of darkness...As I looked far to the rear of this army I saw the entourage of the Accuser himself. I began to understand his strategy, and I was amazed that it was so simple. He knew that a house divided against itself cannot stand, and this army represented an attempt to bring such division to the church that she would completely fall from grace. It was apparent that the only way he could do this was to use Christians to war against their own brethren.

What a terrible sight—Christians marching right along with satan. We must ask ourselves whether we might be some of those who are aligned with the accuser in his attempt to destroy the Church. I want to look just a little further into Joyner's vision so that we might see a little clearer how this warfare is played out.

Trailing behind these first divisions was a multitude of other Christians who were prisoners of this army. All of these were wounded, and were guarded by smaller demons of fear...occasionally, the weaker prisoners would stumble and fall. As soon as they hit the ground, the other prisoners would begin stabbing them with their swords, scorning them as they did this. The vultures would then come and begin devouring the fallen ones even before they were dead. The other Christians prisoners stood by and watched this approvingly, occasionally stabbing the fallen one again with their swords...Then I understood that these prisoners actually thought they were marching in the army of God! This is why they did not kill the little demons of fear, or the vultures—they thought these were messengers from God...They felt that those who stumbled were under God's judgment, which is why they attacked them the way they did—they thought that they were helping God![1]

Have you ever gossiped about some Christian's sin, thinking you were doing God a favor? Have you ever thought that, because something bad happened to a Christian who had sin issues, it was the judgment of God? Therefore, instead of praying for that person, you felt smugly satisfied and openly gossiped about it. Have you ever "stabbed" someone with your sword (words of your mouth), condemning them for a fault? If and when you did these things, you were being employed by the accuser of the brethren. He was using you to keep another brother or sister weak and dejected.

His tactic is to keep us from realizing that we are the children of God. There is nothing more effective at making us feel we are not children of God than having other children of

God gossip about us. Satan's design is to cause us to feel that we are sinners instead of children of God. This demoralization is one of the greatest and most effective tactics of the enemy. Embarrassed and dejected saints wallow in sin because they feel powerless to overcome it. They live lives riddled by guilt, shame, and condemnation.

The Media

The world tells us it is all right to gossip about one another. Newspapers, television, magazines, and the media in general make millions of dollars exploiting individuals. Have you been through the grocery store line and seen the tabloids lately? Slander, gossip, evil reports, and malicious talk are the order of the day. From the bum on the streets to the president of the country, we have no sense of where the charades should end. This society exploits individuals by sharing their misfortunes, sins, and weaknesses. Talk shows never tire of exposing people in order to create a scandalous atmosphere. Likewise, we need not think that courtroom shows are popular because people want to know more about the judicial system.

We are so ingrained and brainwashed into believing that it is permissible to violate one another verbally that it takes a concentrated effort to begin to assume new patterns of thought. The lulling effect of our society's permissive disposition about the private lives of people has had long-ranging effects on our social consciousness. Many have come to view their jobs, their schools, and even their churches as nothing more than a "talk show."

Our words create injury and pain in people's lives, yet we seem oblivious to the destructive results. How often our mouths ramble on casually and carelessly without any thought as to the repercussions we may be causing in other people's lives. Really, we degrade people when we gossip about them. When we finish gossiping about them, we walk away feeling less respect for them than ever, and often we're committed to making others feel the same way. Our own character is perverted by our gossiping when we begin to enjoy denigrating other people. We do all this under a perverted sort of thinking that we are merely "sharing."

Seven Reporters

Thus far we have used the term *gossip* as a cover word for all types of evil reporting. However, let us now give some distinction to the different types of expressions that make up the group of "evil reporters." There are seven types of tongue waggers we should be aware of, and one of them we will deal with in a separate chapter.[2] The last one we will address is the "persecutor." Below I have listed all seven and a general definition of each. See if you can recognize any of them.

1. ***The Backbiter:*** *One who speaks against an absent individual, or a person who is inclined to betray a person when it comes to being loyal.* Backbiters typically have a Judas spirit—the spirit of a "betrayer." As long as they are with you, you are the greatest person on the planet, but after they leave you, they are not loyal to you. You might hear backbiters say, "Your secret is safe with me." But an hour later, your secret is on its way to New York to be broadcasted on national television. The backbiter spirit has caused grief and hurt to many people. The Word of God speaks of the backbiter in Psalm 15:1-3:

> *Lord, who shall abide in Thy tabernacle? Who shall dwell in Thy holy hill? He that walketh uprightly, and worketh righteousness, and speaketh truth in his heart. He that **backbiteth not with his tongue**, nor doeth evil to his neighbor, nor taketh up a reproach against his neighbor.*

Some people are specifically given to this sin. They get a kick out of buddying up with others to obtain information and then using that information to damage their reputation.

2. ***The Busybody:*** *One who is overly involved in the personal lives of other people.* Another definition of a busybody is someone who has a voracious appetite for the personal affairs of others. Life for busybodies is boring if they cannot be involved in other people's business. The busybody is identified in First Peter 4:15. *"But let none of you suffer as a murderer, or as a thief, or as an evil doer, or **as a busybody in other men's matters**."* Please note the severity of the crimes listed here. One would not think that a busybody would be found on the same list as a murderer, thief, and an evildoer. These are crimes people suffer for committing. Yet on this list is also a busybody.

    When people are busybodies, the enemy will cause them to get caught up in things that they normally would never be involved in. Thus the apostle Peter warns us that to be a busybody is to place yourself in the position of being condemned with sinners. Many saints today are suffering as busybodies. They have been injured emotionally, spiritually, or physically because they were at the wrong place at the wrong time and failed to mind their own business.

3. *The Complainer: One who finds fault.* Complainers are people who are perpetually disgruntled. You may hear them say, "I was unfairly treated," "This church is too dirty," or "You didn't do it right." Complainers usually draw a crowd because complainers share from a personal perspective. Their critical complaints and stories embrace the emotions and create an atmosphere of sympathy for their cause. Complainers are identified in Numbers 11:1, *"Now when **the people complained**, it displeased the Lord; for the Lord heard it, and His anger was aroused"* (NKJV). Many people are guilty of having a complaining spirit, even in the Church. Nothing satisfies them, nothing is good enough for them, and nothing pleases them.

We can also find complainers in the Book of Jude. Jude verse 16 says,

> *These are murmurers, **complainers**, walking after their own lust; and their mouth speaketh great swelling words, having men's persons in admiration because of advantage.*

Here, the spirit of the complainer is associated with a person's lust. This would explain why complainers are never satisfied, because lust is never satisfied. Complainers will always be dissatisfied, no matter what you give. I have seen complainers cripple entire churches, dragging them down from spiritual heights with nagging, negative observations. Complainers in the Church should be silenced.

4. **The Murmurer:** *One who grumbles.* The murmurer and the complainer are very similar. There is only one slight difference. Murmuring is associated with an individual. People murmur against a person—usually in leadership—while a complainer focuses on the situation, an institution, or its operation. People can be complainers in their own homes alone, but murmurers have something to say to other people about what someone else is doing. The murmurer spirit is best known for finding fault with leadership and sharing that perspective with others. The poison is then spread into the hearts of others and they also begin to murmur. The hallmark of murmurers is a bad attitude.

Paul identifies the murmurers at Philippi. Philippians 2:14 says, *"Do all things without **murmuring** and disputings."* We can see from this Scripture that murmurers murmur during the work, while complainers express their disapproval before or after the work is done. Murmuring can be very contagious. Once a few people start to murmur, an entire body of people can catch the same spirit. Exodus 16:2 says, *"And the whole congregation of the children of Israel **murmured against Moses** and Aaron in the wilderness."* This is a biblical example, but the same is true concerning many churches today. Often entire congregations are incensed with murmuring. Sometimes an entire workforce can be infected with murmuring.

Moreover, murmurers despise leadership because they are rebellious. The murmuring spirit is a rebellious spirit. It secretly seeks to usurp authority and to rule in the place of rightful authority. Sometimes a wife may despise her husband's godly authority in the home and become a perpetual murmurer, constantly pointing out the faults and weaknesses of her husband. The murmuring spirit is an insidious cancer in many businesses, homes, and churches today.

5. ***The Slanderer:*** *One who tries to injure someone's reputation or character by false or defamatory statements.* Slanderers are more ill-intended than any of those who give an evil report because their aim is to destroy. Slanderers typically work against someone who has attained some degree of recognition or status. People who are slanderers are extremely detrimental because they hurt not only the person being slandered, but they also hurt their families and those who believe in them. Slanderers are brought

out in Jeremiah 6:28, *"They are all stubborn rebels, walking as slanderers..."* (NKJV).

The word *slanderer* means scandal monger. Much of what used to be honest politics in our country has now turned into scandal politics. Scandal politics is where two candidates, both working in their own self-righteousness, seek to malign the other while voters make their decisions on the basis of whether a candidate has come up to standards of human righteousness. If one candidate is slandered, and we find out he smoked marijuana in college or was with a prostitute in his past, we feel like we need to do God a favor and vote him out as if we have never sinned. Let me quickly add that I am not advocating dissolute living in governmental leadership, but the spirit of slander has taken politics far off the mark.

The apostle Paul in his writings mentioned that deacon wives should not be involved in this sin of slander. First Timothy 3:11 says, *"Likewise, their wives must be reverent, **not slanderers**, temperate, faithful in all things"* (NKJV). When the apostle Paul wrote First and Second Timothy, he was laying the foundation for church operation and administration. Therefore, the reference here would be a reference to slanderers in the church. Of all the evil reporting that often goes on in churches, slander in the church can be the most stifling because of the long-ranging effects it can have on ministry.

Let us remember that satan is seeking someone to help him destroy the Church. To speak ill of others may hurt the reputation of someone whom you don't particularly like, but if you could see Christ's tears, you would reconsider.

6. ***The Whisperer:*** *An individual who talks about other people privately, secretly, or covertly.* Most of us have experienced the pain of associating with a whisperer. Whisperers are quiet and unassuming. They may seem innocent, casual, and even innocuous, but their lips are poison. Consider Proverbs 16:28: *"A perverse man sows strife, and a **whisperer separates the best of friends"** (NKJV). Whisperers are different from other evil reporters because they do not try to directly destroy the people they speak evil of, but only to "throw dirt" on them. The dirt, however, is destructive. Whisperers may even first speak well of the individual before they dump their poison.

Here is a good example of a whisperer in the Church. After a Sunday morning worship service, the whisperer walks up to an innocent person who is praising God for the message and says to her, "Pastor Jackson really preached well today, didn't he?" The other person replies, "He sure did, I am so blessed. I needed that message!" Then the whisperer comments as she is walking away, "But you know, they say he mistreats his wife." With statements like this one, whisperers tear away at other people's reputations. Most of the time whisperers will not stop until the entire church is filled with their doctrine. David says in Psalm 41:7, *"All who hate me* **whisper together against me***; against me they devise my hurt"* (NKJV). How many of us have lost friends, business partners, even potential mates because of whisperers.

7. ***The Liar:*** *A person who habitually and intentionally lies or a person who perverts the truth.* Nobody likes liars. How unsettling it is when you can't trust anything people say. That is what it is like to deal with liars. Liars have no integrity. They have lost all sensitivity to the fact that without truth there is no solid ground to stand on. Therefore, if you are dealing with liars, you are never on solid ground. The moment you think you are getting somewhere, you find out that the premise you have been offered is false.

God hates lying since He loves all people. Consider Proverbs 6:16-17, *"These six things doth the Lord hate: yea seven are an abomination unto him: a proud look, a lying tongue...."* Jesus tell us the source of lying in John 8:44: *"Ye are of your father, the devil, and the lust of your father ye will do...when he speaketh a lie, he speaketh of his own: for he is a liar, and the father of it."* The Bible also tells us what will happen to liars when they are judged in Revelation 21:8: *"...and all liars, shall have their part in the lake which burneth with fire and brimstone...."*

Children of God should not be associated with liars and should never be a party to a lie. Let us make it up in our minds that we are going to live life like we are on the witness stand and God is the judge. We shall determine to tell the truth, the whole truth, and nothing but the truth, so help us God.

Although I have taken the time to identify satan as the accuser of the brethren, it is important for us to understand that he does not have control over our tongues. His work is to take advantage of people who do not take control of their tongues. Therefore, we should begin to be more responsible for the conversations we have, understanding our responsibility to our Lord Jesus Christ as His agents in this world.

Runaway Conversation

There is no need for me to give you a thousand illustrations of gossip in everyday life. Most of us are quite acquainted with the accuser and his work of runaway conversations. Let us now take a model conversation as a basic example of a classic runaway conversation. Maybe you can see yourself in it. Michael Sedler, in his book *Stop The Runaway Conversation,* tells of a conversation he had with his supervisor that got out of hand. It is the type of conversation that happens every day to the harm of other people. He writes,

It was a time when I was involved in coaching at the junior high school level. One of the teachers/coaches I worked with was lacking in some areas of responsibility, which made working with him rather tiresome. It was well known among the staff (and even the district) that Jim had an anger problem and was not the most responsible or organized individual. During the course of one week as I was talking with a supervisor about my coaching experience, we began to talk about Jim, and in a joking manner, went through a few of his escapades in the past months and years. As we continued, I began to recount some of my most recent frustrations with Jim, and the supervisor, likewise, shared his frustrations.

Later that evening, as I mulled over my part of the conversation, I realized that I had polluted the supervisor due to my speaking negatively about Jim. Now everything I said was true. He was usually late for practice; he wasn't organized; he left work early; and he did lack certain people skills. However, it was not my place, nor my responsibility to systematically address each of his shortcomings with the clear intent to injure his reputation. Again, I am called to be a light, to speak with a spirit of truth and humility. Yet, as I examined my motivation and my heart, I realize that there was some malice and frustration in my conversation. I had defiled the supervisor and defrauded Jim. I was a whisperer, a complainer, and a slanderer. Worse, I had failed to be a witness of Christianity in the midst of a secular system.[2]

How often have we been in similar types of conversations? Many people, through conversations like this one, on a daily basis destroy friendships, marriages, reputations, and even partnerships. I have found that people who give evil reports about others will often justify their behavior by saying, "Everything I said was true." The general thought is that, if what we are saying about another person is true, we are not doing any wrong;

we are simply "sharing." Notice that in the above story, Sedler acknowledges that the things he said about Jim were true, yet they were nonetheless destructive, and he was nonetheless guilty. Truth or non-truth does not make us any more or less an agent of the accuser. To be Christians in this world requires us to do the entire will of God. God is not looking for saints who will say, "Lord, I was gossiping, but all that I said was true." He's looking for saints who will have holy lips.

Consider Isaiah in his vision of the Lord. God gave Isaiah an open vision, and he was allowed to see the Lord in His glory, sitting on His throne. He cried, *"Woe is me, for I am undone; because I am a man of unclean lips, and I dwell in the midst of a people of unclean lips…"* (Isa. 6:5). The sin that was most prominent to Isaiah was filthy conversation, both his own and that of the people he lived around. He goes on in the same text to show the cleansing power of the Lord concerning the mouths of the saints. He writes:

> *Then flew one of the Seraphims unto me, having a live coal in his hand, which he had taken with the tongs from off the alter: and he laid it upon my mouth, and said, "Lo, this hath touched thy lips; and thine iniquity is taken away, and thy sin purged"* (Isaiah 6:6-7).

May the Lord touch the mouths of the saints that their conversations would be pleasing to God.

Now let us hear Michael Sedler's conclusion to his conversation with his supervisor:

> The next day I contacted the supervisor. I asked for his forgiveness for saying negative things about Jim. His

response was one of shock and confusion. You see, in his eyes we did nothing wrong; we were part of a social setting in which cutting one another down and picking each other apart like vultures was fairly commonplace. He told me there was no need to say I was sorry, but I knew better. I explained that my speaking was not Christlike and did not create a positive environment— nor did it help Jim. After further discussion and testimony, the supervisor thanked me for my willingness to "take a stand." His appreciation for my honesty and intentions to create a godly atmosphere in the workplace were well received. I also developed a new prayer burden for Jim.[3]

Walking in Love

Someone may be asking, "How do I get a grip on my conversation?" Many leaders would suggest that, in order to stop gossiping, we should watch our conversations and make sure we never say anything negative about anyone. That sounds good, but is often problematic. Here's why. Often our conversations do not start off as gossip. They start off as friendly social engagements that turn into "forth telling" and end up as "fortune telling." Sometimes the lines get blurry. We may feel one moment like we are "sharing" with a friend important information about a certain person, and the next moment we feel like we are gossiping.

Then there is the guilt factor. Once we become aware of gossip as a sin, we may begin to feel that we are gossiping anytime we are enjoying a conversation about a third party or receiving information about someone that we did not previously know about. Sometimes we really don't know when we are gossiping and when we are not. Furthermore, we cannot pick and choose our conversations, nor can we control what others will say to us. Thus to simply say "watch our conversations" is good, but inadequate.

As a prelude to my own suggestion as to how to stay out of gossip, I would add that we should absolutely avoid those who are given to gossip and slander. This is the best way to keep from being contaminated. Paul writes in First Corinthians 5:9, *"I wrote unto you in an epistle not to company with fornicators."* This tells us that oftentimes the best way to keep certain sins out of our lives is to not associate with those who do those things. Gossip and evil reporting are the same way. Thus, we should not company or have much conversation with those who make their enjoyment the personal lives of other people. Neither should we take part in the giving or receiving of slander. By doing this, we will keep ourselves pure.

However, this is not the end of the matter, for often gossip is found among the most saintly of individuals. In the preceding story, we would certainly not say that Michael Sedler is someone who is "given" to gossip or someone who "enjoys" slander. No, he is an ordinary Christian just like us. The remedy for gossip cannot be simply to "watch" our conversation. It is good to do that, but it is not always realistic. There are many things we have to think about during the course of a day, not to mention the many suggestions and comments of other people. This makes keeping an ear on our conversation difficult. There are also times we may need to know the information someone shares with us about another person. To listen to something someone wants to tell us is not a sin, and to tell relevant information to someone who needs to know it is also not a sin. Much of what is the sin of the mouth comes down to motives.

What then is my suggestion for keeping our conversations pure and staying free from gossip? Consider this. I have a biological brother named Kerry. I have never gossiped about him to anyone (although I have told my sisters things I am concerned about regarding him). Why is it, do you think, that I have never gossiped about him? It is simply because he is my brother and his personal life is nobody else's business. No matter how atrocious his shenanigans have been, I always shut my mouth about him to others. I pray for him, I talk to him, I may even rebuke him, but I never gossip about him nor glory in his failures and mistakes. Why? Because he is my brother.

The saints have a much stronger connection than biology, although many saints don't know it. The first two words of the Lord's Prayer are *"Our Father…"* not "My Father," but *"Our Father"* (Matt. 6:9). God wants us to realize that we are brothers and sisters in Christ. As Christians, we should have the same disposition about our speech toward each other as I have toward my biological brother. If some saint is out of order, there is an appropriate person to rebuke him. There also must be spiritual ones in the church who have the ministry of restoration, but we must never glory in one another's sin, faults, failures, or mistakes. We should love one another. It was our Lord who spoke these words in John 13:34, *"A new commandment I give unto you, that ye love one another; as I have loved you, that ye also love one another."*

Let me suggest as a solution to the spirit of gossip something that God taught me through Kenneth Hagin that had a profound impact on my life. It is called "walking in love." When we talk about each other, we are failing to realize and recognize the family of God on earth. We must love the brothers and sisters in Christ whom we are familiar with and the ones we are not. We must love the black brothers and sisters in Christ, and we must love the white brothers and sisters in Christ. We must love the rich brothers and sisters in Christ, and we must love the poor brothers and sisters in Christ. We must love the Charismatic or Pentecostal brothers and sisters in Christ, and we must love the Methodist, Presbyterian, Catholic, Episcopalian, Baptist (and so forth) brothers and sisters in Christ. We must love the sanctified brothers and sisters in Christ, and we must love the unsanctified brothers and sisters in Christ. We often gossip about our brothers and sisters who are not yet perfected or sanctified, but that does not make them any less our brothers and sisters in Christ, for even we were at one time or another unsanctified.

Therefore,

Beloved, let us love one another: for love is of God; and everyone that loveth is born of God and knoweth God. He that loveth not, knoweth not God; for God is love.... Beloved, if God so loved us, we ought also to love one another (1 John 4:7-8,11).

I have experienced much more victory over gossip by walking in love toward others than I ever did by "watching" my conversation. At times, when I would be inclined to gossip about someone, the Holy Spirit would say to me, "That is your brother; what you are about to say is not out of love, but judgment." I would immediately repent. Walking in love will move us beyond the issues and give us God's heart for one another. For further study in the area of walking in love toward others, I highly recommend Kenneth Hagin's book, *Love: The Way To Victory.*[4]

Motive

Over the years I have met many saints who wanted to make sure they kept themselves free from the spirit of gossip. As I have given thought and prayer to the matter, the Holy Spirit has led me to understand that much of what constitutes gossip has to do with motive. It all comes down to not necessarily what we say, but why we say it. Gossip is not two people sharing information about a third individual. How do we define gossip? Many of us want to know by strict rules when we are gossiping and when we are not. However, gossip is motive-oriented. Apart from motive, gossip cannot be defined. If I tell my wife, "Our friend Cathy is having an affair," am I gossiping? The answer here would depend on my motive. If I am telling my wife something that is of interest to us both, then what I am sharing is not gossip. Say I pick up the phone and call a friend and ask, "How are Cathy and her husband doing?" Is that gossip? Again the answer would depend on the motive of the call. If I call and ask about Cathy out of a sincere and personal interest in Cathy and her well-being, then it is not gossip. But if I call a friend and ask, "How are Cathy and her husband doing?" with the express purpose of exploiting Cathy's personal life, then it is gossip, and God will hold me accountable for it. What *is gossip* and what *is not gossip* has a lot to do with *motive*.

Casting a Negative Image

Gossip happens when one person seeks to cast a negative image of another person. Here is an example: One woman calls her friend to tell her a few things about her pastor. She says, "Hey girl, did I tell you about my pastor? He has done a wonderful job with the children's ministry. He is preaching well on Sunday mornings, and he is going out of his way to be supportive of elderly members of the church." If we were listening in on this conversation, none of us would say this woman is gossiping. We would say she is sharing with a friend about her pastor. This is why gossip cannot be defined as the sharing of information.

However let us take another situation where one friend calls another. He says, "Hey girl, did I tell you about my pastor? Someone said this week they saw him coming out of the liquor store. They say he gets drunk and his family can't live with him. I heard he has been doing this for years!" Here we have another situation where information is being shared. But this time I think we all would agree that this is gossip. What is the difference between the two?

The difference is that the intention of the latter person is to cast a negative image of the pastor. This constitutes gossip. This is why it all comes down to walking in love. Regardless of the nature of the information we need to share about someone, we should never be the one who is casting a negative image of another person. If we are talking with someone and what we say about a third person would make them look bad, we should hold that information. Jesus said, *"Do unto others as you would have them to do unto you"* (Matt. 7:12). When we speak of someone, we should consider ourselves. If the image we are casting we would not desire for ourselves, then we should not share it with others.

Endnotes

1. Rick Joyner, *The Final Quest* (New Kensington, PA: Whitaker House, 1996), 16-20.

2. Michael Sedler, *Stop The Runaway Conversation* (Grand Rapids, MI: Chosen Books, 2002), 80-86.

3. *Ibid.,* 86-88.

4. Kenneth Hagin, *Love: The Way to Victory* (Tulsa, OK: Faith Library Publications, 1994).

Chapter 3

Why Do People Gossip?

For the heart—assume everything you say about another person, they can overhear; now speak accordingly.

—STEVEN COVEY[1]

AN INTERESTING THING happened to me one day while I was walking through the grocery store. I walked up to a young man whom I had seen before, but had never held a conversation with. As I approached him, I extended my hand and greeted him. The first words out of my mouth were, "Now what is your name? I have seen you before, but I don't think I know you." To my surprise, this young man's response was, "Yeah, but I know you"—spoken in a rather negative tone. I was a bit confused, thinking maybe this was someone I knew in the past, but had forgotten. I questioned him as to when we had previous acquaintance and he said, "We have never had acquaintance. I know you through a friend." As it turned out, this young man had a friend who worked on the same job with me in the past. His friend had shared some gossip about me with him, and he was still using that information in his analysis of me. This friend of his was never a close acquaintance of mine, just a fellow employee working in the same institution.

Through this short conversation, we can see how gossip has lasting effects on people's conscious. Years after I had left that job, this man was still using certain gossip about me in his assessment of me. The utter resoluteness of his expression "I know you" was a good indicator that he both believed that what he was told about me was true and that it still applied. In this way, when we gossip about people, we fail to give them the opportunity to move beyond their mistakes. Gossip is like a person who has a picture of you doing something wrong, and each time you seek to move beyond it, they pull out the picture to remind you of your past, thus leaving you feeling inextricably bound to your mistakes.

What disturbed me most about this incidence was not the gossip nor his inability to move beyond it. What was most shocking to me was that he felt that he "knew me." This, above all else, is the most challenging aspect of the effects of gossip. When the young man said to me, "I know you," the first thought in my mind was, *You may know about me, but you do not know me!* It is utter arrogance to assume that we "know" someone based on what we have heard about them.

To help us understand this, let's look at two biblical characters as examples. None of us were alive during David's lifetime. What if God could send you back to biblical days and plant your feet on the streets of Jerusalem without any of the biblical knowledge that you have now. Then imagine that some people took you into their home and began to tell you about a young man named David. They might say, "There is this young rebel named David who's running from King Saul. He used to play the harp for him, but something bad happened. The people say the king wants him dead. I hope I find him so I can turn him in!" Now what if, a few months later, you happen to see David, and you walk up to him and say, "Hi, Mr. David. You don't know me, but I know you!"

You would be trying to assess David's entire life based on an isolated incident that happened between him and King Saul. You would not be able to see the panorama of David's life, nor appreciate his calling and his relationship to God. Nor could you appreciate the spiritual blessings he would leave us through his writings. You would not, at that point, know that he was a man after God's own heart or that he would be a great king one day. In other words, your only point of reference would be the gossip you heard. The point here is that people's lives cannot and should not be assessed by isolated failures, sins, blunders, or misfortunes. Some Christians daily make value assessments about their brothers and sisters based on what they know about or heard about them through gossip.

Let's take another example. Let's move up in history about 800 years to the days right after Jesus' death. You are living in Samaria with your family and someone approaches you to gossip about a man named Paul. Remember, you have never heard of Paul, so you listen attentively. They say to you, "There is a man named Saul or Paul, I'm not sure, but they tell me none of the Jews like him. They say he is wanted for murder! Yes, he used to kill Christians. But they are saying that to keep the Romans from killing him, he is now posing himself to be a Christian." A few weeks later, you happen to meet Paul, and the first thing you say is, "Hi, Mr. Paul. You don't know me, but I know you!" What a tragedy it would be if you clung so strongly to what you heard about Paul that when you heard him preach you refused to listen to him, believing what you heard about him instead of getting to know him. You would be closing your ears to one of the greatest men of God who ever walked this earth.

Unfortunately, this type of thing goes on every day all around us. All of us have formed opinions about others based on what we heard about them, but we really have never gotten to know them. By doing this, we are essentially trying to reduce their entire contribution to life down to a few isolated experiences. Regardless of what people have gone through or done, they deserve the right to recover and move on with their lives. Saints, let us refuse gossip, and by doing so, allow people to move beyond their history and on into the will of God for their lives.

I have thus far shared some of the spiritual ramifications of gossip. In this chapter, I will identify some reasons why people gossip and give some practical things we can do to keep ourselves free from gossip. The following list is not exhaustive; these are the top reasons I have found that cause people to gossip.

Lack of Effort to Stop

And that ye study to be quiet, and do your own business,
and work with your own hands, as we commanded you
(1 Thessalonians 4:11).

Many people have not ceased to gossip because they have never tried. They have always allowed their flesh to rule and to dictate to them what they will do and say. The above Scripture says, *"study to be quiet."* This means giving attention and diligence to our mouths. If we are going to not talk too much, and if we are going to stop gossiping, we will have to work at it. This

Scripture also says, *"do your own business."* This is the biblical equivalent of a phrase many gossips have heard before, "Mind your own business!" A part of our victory over gossip will be becoming less interested in everyone else's business. Being overly interested in other people's business is a sign that our flesh is undisciplined. The flesh we live in is sinful, and therefore tends to have a natural propensity for the negative, but we have to learn how to mortify our flesh and incline ourselves toward godly things through the Spirit. Without effort and work, we will spend our lives transmitting those things God would rather we never mention.

Offense

Blessed is he, whosoever shall not be offended in Me (Matthew 11:6).

God made us all different. The reality of this sometimes blows our minds. This means that from time to time we are going to meet someone who is different from us. I can even venture to say that we will even meet some people we don't particularly like. What do we do when someone at the office is a bright, happy, and outgoing person, if we are slower and more methodical in our deportment? Do we accept them the way they are? Do we seek to make them act like us? Do we make evil reports that would tarnish someone else's opinion of them?

In life, we will meet people who are different from us. We should make up our minds that we will not be offended if the people we work with or go to church with are not exactly like us. Just think, if Jesus came to earth during our time instead of years ago, would His religious style be the same as ours? If not, would it rub us the wrong way and leave us gossiping about Him on the phone at night?

No one has a right to demand that everyone be just like them. Yet, many Christians are offended every time they meet another Christian who does not see the world the same way they do. Sometimes the spirit of offense can come in during a simple conversation. A person may make a statement we don't appreciate, and we will be faced with a dilemma of whether we will overlook it and forgive, or hold a grudge. To be Christlike and to stay away from gossip, we must decide that we will not allow the spirit of offense to rule. Some saints today have broken relationships in their lives because they have been offended, but healing starts with forgiveness and refusing to hold a grudge.

Retaliation

Not rendering evil for evil or railing for railing: but contrariwise blessing; knowing that ye are therefore called, that ye should inherit a blessing (1 Peter 3:9).

Some have entered the gossip game because they were attacked either verbally or physically. When people verbally assault us, it is a natural response to defend ourselves, but we as believers are not natural beings. We are spiritual beings. The Christian life is not a natural life, nor is it a life of defending ourselves. Our example is Jesus, *"Who when He was reviled* [attacked verbally], *reviled not again; when He suffered, He threatened not; but committed Himself to Him that judgeth rightly"* (1 Peter 2:23). Peter sets Jesus as an example to us of suffering. Peter says that we should not return *"railing for railing."* We can easily see that evil reporting and gossip are like fire spreading its destructive flames on other people. Because some people fight fire with fire, they burn down homes, jobs, leaders, and even churches.

The Christian mandate is to bless and not curse. As children of God, we should take up our ministry of putting gossip to rest by refusing to continue the vicious cycle of gossip. We can put the fires of gossip out by speaking positively about the worst of individuals. We may not like their behavior, but that does not mean we have to hate them. The next time someone is spreading the fire of gossip, find a good word to speak on behalf of the person being talked about and watch the waters of a kind word put out the flames of gossip.

Negative

And be not conformed to this world: but be ye transformed by the renewing of your mind, that ye may prove what is that good, and acceptable, and perfect will of God (Romans 12:2).

Some people are just negative. I mean, they cannot see good in anything. They will scoff at a child being born. Some people are so stuck in the negative that gossip comes naturally for them. Negative minds and gossip are like a car and gasoline. Unless people have a renewed mind, they will trend toward the baser thing of life. Unfortunately, I have found many negative people in the Church—people who sing about Heaven, but who refuse to believe anybody is going there. If you tell them someone is graduating from college, they talk about how there are no jobs available. If you tell them you are getting married, they talk about the likelihood of divorce. If you tell them you got a raise on your job, they start talking about the price of food going up.

They are just negative. Negative people love gossip. It fits their mindsets.

But God is in the blessing business, and He is not looking for a new job. We need to renew our minds. Jesus came to earth to model the ways and means of God. I don't remember anywhere in Scripture where Jesus was negative. When they ran out of wine at the wedding feast, Jesus could have said, "See, I told you they were not going to have enough..." (see John 2:1-3). When the crowd of 5,000 needed food, Jesus could have said, "Some of you are going to have a heatstroke before you get home..." (see John 6:3-5). But that's not Jesus' character, and it should not be ours. Jesus spoke life and blessed people; negative people speak death and curse people.

Widows

But the younger widows refuse...and withal they learn to be idle, wandering about from house to house; and not only idle but tattlers also and busybodies, speaking things which they ought not (1 Timothy 5:11a,13).

In the Book of First Timothy, Paul addresses the matter of widows in the church. Much of what he says about widows has to do with them refraining from the tendency to become gossips. When a woman is older and single, she may seek ways of entertaining herself in the absence of a husband. Paul admonishes the widows to keep from being gossips, tattlers, and busybodies. In the above passage, he addresses the younger widows. These are widows below the age of 60. He instructs Timothy not to receive them as widows to be supported by the church. The reason for his refusal of them was that they had a tendency toward certain sins. What were those sins? Paul writes, *"they learn to be idle, wandering from house to house; and not only idle but tattlers also and busybodies, speaking things which they ought not"* (1 Tim. 5:13). He identifies one of the besetting sins of some widows as the sin of speaking things they ought not.

I have found that the same sins often beset some married women who are older, but immature in the faith. Widows should make themselves useful in taking care of older people, volunteering to give support to godly causes, guiding their grandchildren in the faith, and taking up the ministry of prayer. They should be agents of change in their latter years, determined to influence the world for Jesus Christ.

Jealousy and Envy

But Martha was cumbered about much serving, and came to Him, and said, "Lord doest Thou not care that my sister hath left me to serve alone? Bid her therefore that she help me" (Luke 10:40).

Some people gossip about people to defame them, to hinder or to prevent their admiration and spoil their reputation—especially if they are held in high esteem. Martha decided she would serve Jesus. Mary decided she would listen to Jesus. When Martha noticed that Jesus was impressed with Mary's listening, she became jealous and went to Jesus to defame and gossip about her. She said in essence, "Jesus, let me tell You something about that woman. You don't know Mary like I do. She left me in the kitchen to serve alone. I have been working here all day to get ready for this dinner, and she has not lifted one finger to help me."

What did Martha expect Jesus to do—join her in her gossip? Some people gossip out of jealousy to divulge something about another person that will keep them from being admired or respected. Martha did not want Jesus to admire Mary, so she let Jesus in on one of Mary's faults. Jesus' response to her evil report was:

> *Martha, Martha, thou art careful and worried about many things. But one thing is needful: and Mary hath chosen that good part, which shall not be taken away from her"* (Luke 10:41-42).

Sometimes the people we talk about simply made better choices than we did. They should not be slandered because we work while they have something good going on in their lives.

To Hinder Others

> *For promotion cometh neither from the east, nor the west, nor from the south. But God is the judge: He putteth down one, and setteth up another* (Psalm 75:6-7).

People often gossip to rob a person of the good will of other people. This type of gossip is used as a means of hindering or spoiling a person's success. Practically speaking, you cannot be successful in life without the good will of people. Imagine being an insurance agent when, because of gossip, everyone thinks you're a pervert. Imagine being a teacher when people have spread the word that you are a child molester. Imagine trying to be a contractor when everyone is saying that you will rob people blind. Imagine being a lawyer when people are saying you are incompetent. You may, despite the gossip, be able to function, but to advance in your trade and to reach a point of success, you will need to clear your name.

Gossip is a sure way of hindering a person's success, and many people use it to hinder other people every day. It is the enemy's number one tool for hindering ministry. When gossip is used to hinder, often it is because people are trying to take God's work of judging into their own hands. We are not our brother's judge, and it is not our job to seek to decide who succeeds or who fails in life. God is perfectly able to promote or demote any person.

Furthermore, we should understand that sin is a reproach to a person in and of itself. This means that any person who does not deal rightly will be hindered by their sin regardless of whether they are gossiped about or not. For this reason, we should not speak evil of people with the intention of hindering their progress in life. The only time we should share something negative about people should be to alert others to potential dangers involved in their relationship to those people or to make sure they understand all the potential variables in a matter. Otherwise, our conversation as saints should always be positive. We must remember that promotion comes from neither the east nor from the west; promotion comes from the Lord.

Entertainment

For we hear that there are some which walk among you disorderly, not working at all, but are busybodies (2 Thessalonians 3:11).

Many people gossip as a form of entertainment. Gossip for these people is like experiencing through conversation a real life soap opera. People who gossip for entertainment are normally people who have underdeveloped minds or purposeless lives. If we find gossip entertaining, it is perhaps because we are not doing much with our own lives. Instead, we should read a book, get a hobby, learn a new skill, and make ourselves useful. There is no better entertainment than a life of purpose.

In the Scripture above, it says there were people at Thessalonica who did not have anything to do. The Scripture says they were "busybodies." To be a busybody means exercising ourselves in other people's business. For such people, their daily interest involves exploring what is going on in the lives and personal affairs of other people. Paul infers that the cure for being a busybody is to get a job. He says these saints were *not working at all.* These unemployed saints tended to entertain themselves with the negative experiences and personal lives of other people. Their idle minds became tools for satan to stir up all sorts of confusion.

Many people who may be retired and idle should seek work if having time on their hands makes them overly involved in sin or in other people's business. Even volunteer work is a good outlet for keeping our minds occupied. We can, however, be duly employed and still be a monger of gossip for entertainment. Some of us must realize that we are being used by the accuser as a channel for the dissemination of words that are contrary to the will of God. We will answer one day to God for *every idle word* we speak (see Matt. 12:36-37). There are more constructive ways of entertaining ourselves than gossiping. Once we acknowledge that, half the battle is won. The next step is developing new habits to replace the old ones.

Miserable

Let's be honest. Some people gossip because they are miserable. There is an old adage that says, "Misery loves company." The fleshly nature can get a sadistic joy from the negative circumstances in other people's lives. Some people have become disgruntled about their own failures and disappointments in life and tend to get joy and relief from the thought that others are failing or suffering also. They spread their misery by elevating the misfortunes of other people through gossip. I have found that happy people gravitate toward other happy people, and miserable people gravitate toward other miserable people. If your friends or associates are extremely miserable and love to rail on other people, then perhaps you are the same way. If your life is headed downhill, change your attitude, and then change the crowd you hang out with.

Gossiping out of misery has another interesting element. People can get to the point where their lives seem more sane and stable based on the calamities in the lives of other people. For example, the gossip may think, "Mrs. Thomas and her husband broke up, but I still have my husband." At a time when we should be praying for reconciliation, deliverance, and financial grace for another person, we are often glorying in another saint's misfortune. It feels good to tell of the bad that happens to other people, because those bad things are not happening to us. But blessed be the saint who is mature enough to declare about other people: "Though things in their lives are not going very well right now, I am praying for them, and they will come through this by my intercession."

Categorizing People

In our subconscious minds, we tend to place people in categories. We do this in order to make life more safe and sane. We classify people primarily in three basic categories: "good people," "bad people," and "people we don't know anything about." The last group is self-explanatory; we pass by people every day whom we don't know anything about. Whenever we hear something bad about a person, we have an inherent need to categorize them as "bad" in our minds. If we hear from a friend that a certain woman is treacherous, or if we hear that a certain man is dangerous, we label them as bad in our minds. This is quite natural and not altogether wrong. We do this to protect ourselves from danger. We learn this behavior as children. When we were young and met other kids who did bad things, we learned to avoid them (unless we were one of the ones doing bad things). The Bible also teaches us to separate from those who do not do the will of God.

We can, however, become so inclined to categorize people that we become self-righteous. When we come into Christ, it is easy to inappropriately classify and categorize people in negative ways. For instance, a person may hear that another person has been to jail for embezzlement, and immediately he places that person in the "bad" category in his mind. From that point on, his relationship with that person is affected by this knowledge. Then the same person hears someone say that a certain other person is a dedicated family man and an officer in the church, and he places that person in the "good" category in his mind.

The only problem with this is that there is some bad in the best of us, and there is some good in the worst of us. Moreover, if we place the good person under the same circumstances that the bad person has been through, he might not come out in the good category. I am not against being safe and staying away from people we believe to be untrustworthy. I am only saying that we should not be too quick to classify anyone. Even though we may not have heard the best about a person, we should believe for the best. If we have the courage to take some of the people we have in the bad category of our minds out and allow them by faith to be placed in our good category, we will begin to see good in them. They might even become a blessing to us.

Matthew 9:10 says, *"And it came to pass, as Jesus sat at meat in the house, behold, many publicans and sinners came and sat down with Him and His disciples."* In the Jewish mind, publicans and sinners were in the "bad" category, but Jesus chose to see them in faith. He saw good where others saw bad. He refused to allow the evil report about them (whether true or false) to cause Him to stop believing that people could do better and be better.

Categorizing Ministers

It is interesting to note that, although the Holy Spirit inspired the Bible, He does not omit any of the faults or sins of the men and women who are written about. We are told frankly that Moses was a murderer before his calling. The story of David committing adultery is told in great detail. Similarly, people like Abraham, Paul, Peter, and many others are shown to be both spiritual enough to be people of God and yet human enough to have weaknesses. I think this tells us something about God. It certainly tells us that God does not use human perfection as His source of self-esteem. This is important for us to know. God is certainly not looking to us for moral encouragement. We are His children, not His colleagues.

Yet sometimes in our religious fervor we begin to view people of God as if God is looking to them for self-esteem. When a minister of God has a fault or weakness, we may be revolted or shaken by it, but God is not. For this reason, many people in their immature thinking have created two bipolar classes of ministers: (1) the ministers who are perfect and have never done anything wrong and (2) the ministers who are imposters posing as true servants of God. Using these two categories, these people try to make sense of Christian ministry by placing every minister they meet into one of these two categories. They meet a certain pastor, and they think he's perfect and has never made a mistake or sinned. They hold him in high esteem. Then one day they see this same minister buying a lottery ticket, and they begin to gossip about him. Their gossip may sound like this, "You know that pastor that serves at that church on Maple Street. He says he is a man of God, but you know what, he's not a man of God. I saw him with my own two eyes buying a lottery ticket." Many other saints buy into these two extreme categories of ministers. Therefore, the person responding to this gossip may say, "What? My sister goes to his church! I am going to call her tonight; she needs to find another church."

Because we trust more in our categories than we do the Word of God, many saints run from church to church looking for the perfect pastor. Now, I would add that the Word of God is clear that pastors and leaders are to live holy lives as an example to the flock. However, the need to place pastors into two categories of either being saints or raving wolves causes many saints to lose their sensitivity to the humanness of their leadership. Television has made the matter worse, taking every chance it gets to expose any fault or inconsistency in ministers' lives, reinforcing these polar categories.

The truth is, good ministers can have bad faults. If they do not seek God about it and get victory over their weaknesses, it will affect their ministry and ultimately their livelihood. Immoral ministers who will not turn from sin should be removed from the pulpit, and a church cannot tolerate certain sins in leadership.

However, even when we reject people as leaders, we should remember that they are still our brothers and sisters in the Lord. Too many saints falsely believe that all the ministers they have in their "bad" category are not their brothers in Christ. These ministers may not be the best people to lead our churches, but if they have been born again, they are going to the same Heaven as we are. These ministers may have had affairs or took some money or lost their tempers, but think about all the bad things the rest of us have done. We have all had to ask God to forgive us for many things, and He always does. Remember, God does not put us in categories because of our mistakes. He loves us just the same.

To Feel Better About Our Own Faults

This reason is a very prevalent reason why people gossip. Many Christians have sins and weaknesses they privately wrestle with. Instead of looking to God for victory, they justify their own sins by comparing themselves to other Christians who wrestle with "worse" sins. Then, in an effort to feel better about themselves, they spend much time rehearsing the sins of those who are doing things they consider to be worse. For instance, one saint may have the vice of smoking. He knows he needs victory in this area. But instead of keeping his focus on himself, he seeks to lift his discouragement by discussing some other person who happens to be a closet alcoholic. This saint may then temporarily feel better about himself because he is not as "deep in sin" as is this other person.

I happen to know of an entire office building of people who come to work every day and the main order of conversation is the personal lives of other people in the office. Once this type of behavior becomes normative in any place of business, the accuser takes advantage of the situation. The accuser's job is to cause the people involved to subconsciously feel that the only way to "overcome" and to "have victory" in a verbally malicious environment is to prove that the personal lives and sins of other people are worse than their own. The accuser causes people to increase their gossip against other people in the office in an effort to suppress their guilt over what has already been said about their own lives. This type of situation creates a hostile work environment. Once a competitive gossip spirit sets in, all other types of vices ensue.

In some places of employment and in some churches, the gossip is simply out of control. I know of one place of employment where a group of women from the job gathered together to gossip about another woman working in a certain office whose husband was cheating on her. What was ironic about this situation was that they barely knew the woman. The source of their information was also unreliable. This woman's husband did not work at this office, and there was absolutely no legitimate reason for these women to be discussing her. The conversation was simply to exploit this woman's personal life. A few hours later, the woman who was being gossiped about heard about the discussion. In retaliation, she led a group of women on her lunch break in a gossip session about the personal life of one of the female bosses who was involved in the discussion about her husband. Under these types of circumstances, the objective of everyone becomes making sure they are not the subject of the gossip. To ensure that they are not, they make sure they keep gossiping about others.

Instead of continuing in this pattern of negative speech, people (especially Christians) should decide that they will not listen to nor hear any more negative reporting about anyone. Healing cannot occur until people decide to refuse to keep hurting others. We should take an attitude that says, "Let them gossip about me, but it stops with me. I will no more be party to bringing harm to anyone else with my mouth!" It is time for people who say they are believers to act like it somewhere else besides in church.

When we gossip and backbite one another, we are feeding our flesh. The Bible says, *"He that soweth to his flesh, shall of the flesh reap corruption..."* (Gal. 6:8). The corruption in this case is the disintegration of unity on the job. Through allowing the flesh to dominate, many have destroyed the business environment on the job and the spiritual environment in the church, and they have brought hindrances to their own spiritual progress. According to Psalm 133:1-3, the oil of the anointing and the blessing are released when there is unity among people. We will never have unity in businesses, churches, or any organizations filled with gossips, slanderers, whisperers, complainers, and evil reporters.

Self-Esteem

And He spake this parable unto certain which trusted in themselves that they were righteous, and despised other: "Two men went up into the temple to pray; the one a Pharisee, and the other a publican. The Pharisee stood and prayed thus with himself, 'God, I thank Thee, that I am not as other men are, extortioners, unjust, adulterers, or even as this publican. I fast twice in a week, I give tithes of all that I possess.' And the publican, standing afar off, would not lift up so much as his eyes unto heaven, but smote upon his breast, saying 'God be merciful to me a sinner.' I tell you, this man went down to his house justified rather than the other: for everyone that exalteth himself shall be abased; and he that humbleth himself shall be exalted" (Luke 18:9-14).

I have just shared the reality that some people gossip about others because it makes them feel better about their own faults. In a similar way, some people gossip to increase their sense of self-worth. The difference here is that those who gossip about others to feel better about their own faults are fighting low self-esteem, while there is another group who gossip because it can be a negative source of high self-esteem. This latter group is made up of people who want to feel superior to others, but need some sort of criterion for justifying their superiority. These people will use the weaknesses they see in other people as a proof or evidence that they are "better" people. They make social standards and moral standards their guideposts for determining who should be respected and who is important. The people who gossip for self-esteem love to relay the weaknesses of other people. Each time they do, they feel more and more superior. What they fail to realize is that they, like the Pharisee in the text above, are guilty of the worst sin—the sin of pride and self-righteousness.

Dirty Minds

Unto the pure all things are pure: but unto them that are defiled and unbelieving is nothing pure; but even their mind and conscience is defiled (Titus 1:15).

Some people gossip because they have dirty minds. Their minds are full of pornographic and unrighteous thoughts. Because of this, they are only interested in the baser lives of other people. They love to know who is doing what with whom. Their minds are like trashcans, consuming the dirt from the lives of everyone around them. If our minds are trashcans, we will be receptive to dirt. If our minds are pure, we will view things as pure. Noble people tend to view other people as noble. Thieves tend to view other people as thieves. People with dirty minds tend to view other people's lives as dirty. The state of our own minds has a great effect on how we view others.

Romans 12:2 says we are to "renew our minds" with the Word of God. Being Christians does not automatically mean our minds are renewed. Too many Christians are hiding behind Christ to keep people from seeing that their minds are trashy. If we are to be effective witnesses for Christ and assets to the Kingdom of God, we will have to have pure minds. Sometimes gossip is simply a reflection of the trashiness of the person doing the gossiping.

Exaggeration

But let your communication be, "Yea, yea"; "Nay, nay": for whatsoever is more than these cometh of evil (Matthew 5:37).

To exaggerate means to enlarge beyond normal or to overstate. When it comes to talking and sharing, many people fail to realize that it is dishonest not to retell a story or situation in exactly the manner that it happened—and in the spirit that it happened. Exaggerators are people who can augment and embellish any story to make the events seem more glorious, pitiful, lovely, ardent, or in general worse or better than it actually was. Exaggerators tend to have vivid imaginations. They become emotional when retelling events, and their fanciful imaginations take over. When exaggerators hear a person expressing a minor disappointment with someone else, they will make it their responsibility to express that disappointment to the person who caused it. However, by the time they retell the story to the person who was the cause of the disappointment, they will make it seem like the person was so disappointed that he or she may die from grief.

Exaggerators are especially bad in church. If the choir makes a few mistakes, they go out and tell others that the music at church was a complete fiasco. If the minister says something offensive in his sermon, they rush out to tell others, making a slip of words by the minister seem like a verbal attack on the congregation. In the above Scripture, the Lord Jesus tells His disciples that their words should be *"'Yea, yea' and 'Nay, nay,' for whatsoever is more than this cometh of evil."* It is evil to exaggerate. Many saints would do well to learn this. If a person was a little upset, then we should testify that they were a little upset. If the bride's dress was not very pretty in our opinion, then we should just say it was not beautiful to us. If two people had a heated exchange of words, we should just say they had a disagreement and not infer that it was World War III. If we are recounting to someone something we saw or heard, we must tell the truth without adding or inferring anything that was actually not there or did not actually happen. Let our "yea" be "yea" and our "nay" be "nay," for anything more than "yea" and "nay" is of evil.

Information Specialist

There is still one other aspect of gossip that needs to be clarified. Gossip does not have to be one person talking personally about another. Gossip can be defined as idle talk that has no specific objective. I have met many people who were given to gossip who would not consider themselves gossips. They aimlessly talk about people around them, but the talk is void of purpose.

There was a certain nurse who worked with me who had a critical spirit. She was always telling anyone at the office what she knew about any employee who was doing anything wrong. Let me quickly add that telling something that is being done wrong is not a bad thing. But this particular woman was always sharing information with people who did not need to know it.

She might tell a counselor, "Some of these nurses don't carry out procedures like they should. I saw Darlene taking blood without washing her hands." If this information was for the purpose of maintaining hospital standards, it would have been commendable. However she was telling a counselor this information—someone who had nothing to do with nursing. Later she would be talking to a chaplain. She would tell the chaplain how sloppy the nursing manager was, and how it should be a crime for anyone's office to look like a pigpen.

Even though this woman was not telling personal information, she was gossiping nonetheless. This sort of gossip must be realized and acknowledged. This same nurse was fired from her job for telling a patient things about the hospital staff that were confidential. I call this type of behavior self-destructive. When our propensity to gossip causes us difficulty on our job, in our church, or with our friends, it's time for us to change.

Let me give one other incident that is important to this observation of gossip being "information oriented." When I was in school, I had a supervisor whom I had to meet with weekly. She was a Christian woman who loved God deeply. However, she had a vice. She had a tendency, whenever I was in her office, to talk about her colleagues. She would even talk about other students. I would come into her office and sit, and she would say, "You know, I get so tired of certain men. You know the insecure type, like Rayman Bird. He is such a pig." I was a student, and Mr. Bird was a professor, so there was no reason she needed to tell me about him.

But people with loose lips don't realize they are gossips. In fact, this woman presented the information as if it were an opportunity for us to bond. It was like she was "letting me in" on professor stuff. Later in the semester, I would go to her office, and she would bring up other students in the class, saying they were "trifling" or "stupid." I would laugh with her and finish my time wisely. However, I was always told that "if a dog will bring a bone, he will carry one." This is why I was not surprised when a fellow student told me that this same woman said that I was "inconsistent."

This woman probably would not have considered herself a gossip, but she was one, without a doubt. Her self-destructive behavior caused her to lose respect among the students and staff. Over the years, her respect around the institution waned. She would argue that she didn't get the respect because she was a woman. The ironic thing is that I don't think she ever figured out that her mouth was the source of the disrespect.

Nosey

Finally, there are those people who contribute to the gossip community because they are interested in everything. Some people are just nosey. A friend of mine told me once that she and her husband were out of town and she received a call from a certain neighbor who kept up with everybody's business. The neighbor called and said, "I didn't see you or your husband sitting out on the porch yesterday, so I called your son-in-law to find out where you were." My friend replied, "We're doing fine; we're on vacation." The woman said, "Where are you guys? And what are you doing?" My friend was angry at the woman and told her that she didn't have time to talk. The woman realized she had upset her, but to help to make it right, she said, "Well,

I just want to tell you that a tree limb fell in your yard and that your grandson was playing in your flowerbed yesterday. But I will talk with you later."

This woman is a great example of someone who is just nosey, the kind of person who cannot tolerate not knowing something. This is not godly. Everyone has some level of curiosity, but when we allow our flesh to have unrestrained interest in everything and everyone, we have yielded to the flesh. Here is something we all must learn to accept: *We don't have to know everything!* There are some things we will need to know in life, but there are things we can live without knowing. If we are nosey, we must start practicing self-discipline. The Lord will help us. Nosey people make everyone around them miserable because they won't let them live their own lives.

The Rumor Mills

There are places that promote gossip. These are places that we want to avoid or be careful when in attendance. I call them "rumor mills." They are places like barbershops, beauty salons, teacher's lounges, break rooms, and sometimes church halls. While these are places where people given to sinning with their tongues gather, they are also great places where we can be a witness for Jesus. Those who get delivered from sins of the mouth should make their visits to these places an opportunity to share the love of Jesus Christ. Imagine what would happen if, in our beauty salons or barbershops, a positive perspective of the Church would be presented consistently instead of a negative commentary on what the preacher did wrong or what negative thing has happened in someone's life. We should become agents for Christ in the places where satan has consistently ruled.

Telephones and cell phones are also tools of the rumor mills. Today, the internet has expanded the field of gossip through social networking. Websites like Facebook and Twitter can be very useful for good, or they can be used for destructive purposes. We must make up in our minds that our telephones, cell phones, and the internet will no longer be used by the accuser to destroy the saints, but to build up the Body of Christ.

Endnote

1. Steven R. Covey, *The 8th Habit: From Effectiveness to Greatness* (New York, NY: Free Press, 2005), 58.

Chapter 4

Gossip in the Church

You won't become a saint through other people's sins.

—ANTON CHEKHOV[1]

Understanding Righteousness

The Church must never forget its mission. Jesus said we are to be *"fishers of men"* (see Matt 4:19). The Church's work is first and foremost that of saving the sinner. This is dirty work. In the same way that fish don't come out of the water already cleaned, sinners don't come out of the world already sanctified. Luke 15:1-2 says:

> *Then drew near unto Him all the publicans and sinners for to hear Him. And the Pharisees and scribes murmured, saying, "This man receiveth sinners, and eateth with them."*

It was Jesus' custom to receive sinners. Unfortunately, many Christians have lapsed into an attitude that they don't want to get their hands dirty with the sins or sinners of the world. It is a tragedy that today we have churches that only want to take in mature (clean) Christians. Our sense of evangelism has lapsed into pride and arrogance. This is often the reason why there is so much gossip within the Church. Churches that pride themselves on the pristine nature of their members and how they are "upstanding" members of the community will become intolerant of any saints who struggle with sin. Because they believe righteousness is a product of their own works, they stumble when they see their brothers and sisters failing in their moral lives.

Many people gossip about their brothers and sisters in Christ because they don't understand righteousness. They simply don't understand that righteousness is a gift from God to people. They have a legalistic perspective of righteousness. To them, they are righteous because of the good deeds that they do or the bad deeds that they don't do. But righteousness by the law always leaves us feeling either extremely arrogant or totally discouraged depending on how well we are living or with whom we are comparing ourselves. We are encouraged when comparing ourselves to someone we know who is a rank sinner. But we feel bad when we find people who are really on fire for God and seem not to have the slightest struggle with sin.

Regardless of how we feel about our personal state of righteousness, the Scriptures declare, *"For all have sinned, and come short of the glory of God"* (Rom. 3:23). People who have a law-based perspective of righteousness tend to "throw dirt" and gossip about the sins of others because it makes them feel more righteous or holy. They revel in being able to say they saw another Christian doing something wrong. Each time they do, they feel more acceptable with God. They must learn that true righteousness is not of works, but of faith. When Paul got this revelation, he wrote:

But what things were gained to me, those I counted loss for Christ. Yea doubtless, and I count all things but loss for the excellency of the knowledge of Christ Jesus my Lord: for whom I have suffered the loss of all things, and do count them but dung, that I may win Christ, And be found in Him, not having my own righteousness, which is of the law, but that which is through the faith of Christ, the righteousness which is of God by faith (Philippians 3:7-9).

People who understand righteousness by faith know that they are righteous, but they also know that they did not earn it by their good deeds. Therefore, they are not in a competition with other Christians to prove who is the most righteous or most holy. Nor are they overwhelmed with interest in other people's sins. This alleviates the need to gossip about the faults of others. This principle of bequeathed righteousness is seen so vividly in Isaiah 54:17:

"No weapon that is formed against thee shall prosper; and every tongue that shall rise against thee in judgment thou shalt condemn. This is the heritage of the servants of the Lord, and their righteousness is of Me," saith the Lord.

The writer of Isaiah 54:17 was under attack. He declares that the weapons his enemies are employing against him will be ineffective. What are the weapons being used against him? He tells us that the chief weapon being used by his enemies is their tongue.

This familiar passage of Scripture is actually one where a man of God is being attacked verbally—maliciously gossiped about. He is probably facing slander and gossip against his character.

Gossip is an effective weapon. Evil reports are both distracting and discouraging. Here Isaiah appeals to God for help, and he writes this Scripture by the inspiration of the Holy Spirit. The last line of the verse is the most important one here. He writes, *"...and their righteousness is of me' saith the Lord."* We should pay close attention to the text here. The first part of the verse is Isaiah speaking about his accuser's deeds, but in the latter part of the verse Isaiah quotes what God has revealed to him in response to his accusers. He prays to God about the tongue scourging he is receiving from his enemies, and God sends him a rhema word. God says to Isaiah, "Your righteousness is from Me!" Wow, that's powerful!

Here is the situation. Perhaps this man of God has committed some sin, and his enemies hear of it. They are now running his name down, and people everywhere are speaking evil of him. He is deep in prayer about it, and God says, "Isaiah, your righteousness is not your own; it is from Me." Here is an unspoken rule of gossip: Don't gossip about moral people. If we do, we will be condemned because everyone will know that we seek to malign moral people. However, if those moral people are ever caught in an immoral act, we are free to rail on them at will—according to the rules of gossip.

Isaiah, in the text above, obviously has lost all claims to human righteousness. He has sinned and fallen short of the glory of God. He cannot claim innocence. Therefore, he does not, like David, declare that his enemies falsely accuse him. Since Isaiah cannot vindicate himself, God grants him justification. His enemy's weapons still will not prevail against him, not because

Isaiah is righteous, but because God says to him, "I know you failed, and I know you have sinned, but I have enough righteousness for Me and you too." Hallelujah! No wonder Paul could write in Romans 5:17:

> For if by one man's offense death reigned by one; much more they which receive abundance of grace and the gift of righteousness shall reign in life by one, Jesus Christ.

If the Church would realize that the quest for righteousness is over, we could forgive our brothers and sisters and set them free. As long as we are trying to fulfill God's mandate for righteousness in our own strength, we will always have our rulers out measuring how much sin the members have in their lives. But thanks be to God that is over. I have been made righteous by the blood of the crucified Savior. My righteousness is perfect and immutable. I don't have to compare myself to any person because human righteousness is not what God is looking for. Because my righteousness was given to me by God's grace, it is silly of me to speak evil of people who have not yet received their righteousness from God. My job is not to talk about them, but to teach them what God has offered them by grace. Every saint should know Second Corinthians 5:21, *"For He hath made Him to be sin for us, who knew no sin, that we might be made the righteousness of God in Him."*

The Tongue

The Book of James in the New Testament is the only book of the Bible where a pastor is writing a sermon to his local congregation. By a perusal of the book, we can easily see some of the issues James faced in his church. In chapter 3 we learn that one of the major issues the church faced was gossip. There had obviously developed in the Jerusalem church a strong tendency in the saints to gossip about one another. I want to take a brief examination of that portion of the sermon to see what James had to say to his gossiping congregation.

> *Even so the tongue is a little member, and boasteth great things. Behold how great a matter a little fire kindleth. And the tongue is a fire, a world of iniquity: so is the tongue among our members, that it defileth the whole body, and setteth on fire the course of nature; and is set on fire of hell* (James 3:5-6).

These are the powerful words James uses to address his congregation. He begins by reminding them that the tongue, although it is a small member of the body, carries great influence and authority. He compares the tongue to a fire. This analogy is set forth so that the congregation would understand that just as a small fire burns down an entire forest, so does a little gossip destroy an entire church. James is reminding his congregation that they cannot be casual about gossip; they must take a stand against it. The saints often view gossip as a small matter to their own peril. James also adds that the tongue *"is set on fire of hell."* He uses this statement to show his congregation that satan is the author of and authority over reckless tongues. Hell delights to see saints who take gossip and evil reporting as something to joke about.

We should also note the power of the tongue in shaping the lives of our loved ones. Many people today are still trying to overcome the negative words that were spoken over their lives by their parents, grandparents, or some significant other. For example, many people can testify that they were told by a boyfriend, girl-friend, or parent that they were ugly or stupid, and years later they are still going to great efforts to prove to themselves and others that those words are not true. Words are powerful. The Word of God says in Proverbs 18:21 that *"death and life are in the power of the tongue."* What we say to our spouses, children, friends, church members, and so forth has long-lasting effects on them. Let's speak life.

> *For every kind of beast, and of birds and of serpents, and of things in the sea is tamed, and have been tamed of mankind: But the tongue can no man tame; it is an unruly evil, full of deadly poison. Therewith bless we God, even the Father; and therewith curse we men, which are made after the similitude of God. Out of the same mouth proceedeth blessing and cursing. My brethren these things ought not so to be* (James 3:7-10).

James continues his sermon on the tongue by emphasizing to the congregation that we are not able to tame our tongues without the assistance of the Holy Spirit. Whereas in earlier verses he compared the tongue with a fire, in this passage he asserts that the tongue is *"full of deadly poison."* By this he means that gossip kills. It kills vision. It kills reputation. It kills hopes and dreams, and it kills ministry. Negative speech about others is like spreading deadly poison, killing all the creativity and vitality in individuals. Then James says that out of the same mouth we bless God the Father and curse people who are made after the image of God. Maybe James had seen one of his choir members singing high notes about the glory of God, then gossiping low notes about other members of the congregation. James' admonition to this congregation was that *"these thing ought not so to be."* If we have given our lives to God, our tongues also belong to God. Our bodies are the temple of God (see 1 Cor. 6:19). That means that our tongues should be used for the glory of God.

Pastor James does not end his message on the tongue in chapter 3. In the next chapter, he picks up this theme again in verse 11. He writes:

> *Speak not evil one of another, brethren. He that speaketh evil of his brother and judgeth his brother, speaketh evil of the law, and judgeth the law: but if thou judge the law, thou art not a doer of the law, but a judge. There is one lawgiver, who is able to save and destroy: who art thou that judgest another?* (James 4:11-12).

These are such profound words that James speaks—words that many church members need to hear. So many saints have become insensitive to God's displeasure with their speaking evil of others. We can surmise by reading the above text that James' congregation had its share of evil reporting going on. There were probably those in his congregation who were gossiping about the sins of other saints. They probably felt their gossip was justified in the sight of God. But the word from God through this pastor is emphatic—do not speak evil of your brother or sister in Christ.

When we gossip about other saints, we are placing ourselves in the position of being judge in their lives. James says that when we speak evil of other believers, we are saying that we are good enough to be judged by the law. In essence, James is saying that the reason why one person may gossip about another is because he or she keeps a certain aspect of the law that another person breaks. We usually gossip about someone who breaks that portion of the law that we keep. Thus, we feel that we have the right to talk about them.

The law, however, is a unit—like a chain. If we break any part of the law, we break the whole law. James 2:10 says, *"For whosoever shall keep the whole law, and yet offend in one point, he is guilty of all."* Therefore, it does not matter if one person commits adultery and another person steals; they both have broken the whole law. For this reason, we do not have the right to judge another person simply because the part of the law another person breaks is the part we happen to keep. We are not any better because we are walking in victory in an area that another saint is not. We need to praise and pray. Praise God that it is not us who is sinning, and pray for our brother or sister in Christ.

Condemnation

The word *condemnation* comes from the root word *condemn.* This word means to declare to be wrong, to convict of guilt, to sentence judicially, or to pronounce as unfit. The word *condemn* is a word we often hear referred to in judicial matters. We may say that a criminal was condemned and sentenced to death. There is also a type of condemnation that is associated with the Christian life: it is called spiritual condemnation. Spiritual condemnation is when Christians condemn themselves continually because of their past or because of habitual sins. Condemnation is a serious problem for many saints today. Some Christians are in a constant state of guilt because they have committed certain sins or because they fail to be able to find freedom from certain weaknesses.

Millions of people every day live in a never-ending cycle of hopelessness and despair because they cannot forget about yesterday. They are tormented by bad memories that can lead to depression, mental anguish, and even thoughts of suicide. Satan is aware of our condemnation and uses our mistakes to torture and entrap us. One of satan's greatest weapons against Christians is their past. If a sense of guilt and shame over past sins lingers over children of God, they will fail to realize their position in Christ. Furthermore, they will lack the faith to stand on the promises of God and believe God for the things they desire.

Many saints even drift away from church and deeper into the clutches of the enemy because of condemnation. When condemnation sets in, the accuser takes advantage, keeping weary saints in a constant state of doubt and defeat. Outwardly, they look the same and maybe even talk the same as other Christians, but the guilt over secret sin is subverting their faith and destroying their walk with the Lord. To add insult to injury, the accuser works to expose their secret sins to others so that other Christians would assist him in his assault on the weary saints. Before long, these self-condemned saints inherit a host of other saints who support their self-condemnation by constantly gossiping about and reminding them of their faults.

What is the solution to this awful situation? How can we extricate the saints from feeling like they can't study the Word or pray? The answer is not found in some profound revelation of Scripture, but in the very basics of faith. The solution to our problem of self-condemnation is to learn the power of the blood of Jesus. When we condemn ourselves for sin, we are standing in agreement with the accuser. God said in His Word that Jesus died for our sins. Through self-condemnation we are declaring that He did not. When we side with the enemy, we will always feel condemned because satan is already condemned. Pastor Benny Hinn, in his book, *The Blood,* gives us an interesting yet typical story that will heighten our awareness that self-condemnation is quite prevalent among the saints:

> Two years after I began in the ministry, I received a letter that I will never forget from a lady who was extremely distraught. Although her letter did not provide many details, she wrote, "Please pray for me. I feel so horrible about the things I have done that I can't go on. I feel so guilty I just want to commit suicide." My secretary reached her by phone and transferred the call to me…Then I asked, "Why are you so troubled that you want to end your life?" "I am ashamed to admit it," she said, "but I have committed adultery. I slept with five men, and the guilt I feel is so great that I just want to die." "Are you born again?" I inquired. "Yes," she said. My immediate response was, "Have you repented? Have you asked the Lord to forgive you of your sin?" "Yes, I have," she said. "Do you believe God has forgiven you?" There was silence on the other end of the line for a moment. Hesitating, she finally replied in a quiet voice. "I'm not sure." "If we truly repent of our sins, the blood of Christ totally cleanses us. Our past is erased. He not only forgives, but he has also chosen to forget our sins."

The conversation between Pastor Hinn and this woman continued until he said these words.

> "Lady, listen to me…there's a bigger sin you must repent of. Do you realize that you have been grieving the Holy Spirit? It's the sin of not believing God's promises. He

forgave you of your sins…when you prayed and asked him to forgive you. But the devil has used this thing against you… Quit insulting our wonderful Lord and the work of the cross by not accepting what he did for you." She said, "But my sins are so great." "The power of His blood to forgive and reconcile you back to God is greater. Every time you say, I don't believe Jesus will forgive me of my sin, you are going against what the Word of God promises…"[2]

This story is very typical in the Body of Christ. The woman speaking to Pastor Hinn had been in condemnation for 28 years. The accuser had used this yoke to keep her away from church, prayer, and the study of God's Word. Today, too many saints are missing in action (MIA) because of self-condemnation.

I want to point out one important thing we must understand about condemnation. The basis of self-condemnation is often the assumption that once people are saved, they should not have a desire for or weakness to sin. This false assumption leads many to feel that there must be something wrong with their salvation. When they find themselves victims of the sins of their past, some lose hope in their salvation, while others simply resign themselves to not advancing in the Christian life. Whether our sins occurred before or after our salvation, the blood of Jesus is effectual at washing and cleansing us from all unrighteousness. First John 1:9 says, *"If we confess our sins He is faithful and just to forgive our sins and to cleanse us from all unrighteousness."*

We are tripartite beings—body, soul, and spirit. With our bodies we contact the physical realm. Our soul includes our mind, our will, and our emotions. With our souls we contact the intellectual realm. Our spirit is the God part of us. With our spirits we contact the spirit realm. When God saves us, He recreates our human spirits and the Holy Spirit comes to live within us. But what happens to our souls and our bodies? After we are saved, our souls and our bodies are our first assignment. Romans 12:1-2 tells us exactly what is to happen to the soul and the body. Before we consider this Scripture, we should note that the admonition here is not to God, but to the saints. Romans 12:1 tells us what is to happen to our bodies:

> *I beseech you therefore, brethren, by the mercies of God, that ye present your bodies a living sacrifice, holy, acceptable unto God, which is your reasonable service.*

This *"living sacrifice"* simply means that our flesh must die. Romans 12:2 tells us what we must do with our souls. *"And be not conformed to this world: but be ye transformed by the renewing of your mind...."* This means that we are to get our minds (or souls) filled with the Word of God. This is the assignment of every born-again believer.

God is aware that this work is not going to be done over night and that we often have sins that nag us long after we are saved. We press toward the mark of the high calling of God even though we have not yet apprehended. To stand in condemnation is to say, "I can't change, even though God says I can." We must realize that God desires us to press toward perfection. We must also know that He has forgiven us for the blunders we make while on our way there. Victory over sin will be ours if we refuse to agree with satan. It doesn't matter how many times we have fallen; the blood of Jesus will not fail to wash away our sins and give us a new start. Someone once said that God is the

God of a second chance, and maybe that is true. But in my life, He has been the God of the 500th chance. I don't mean that we as Christians should intentionally disrespect the grace of God by willfully sinning, but often we fail more than once or twice before we overcome.

I want to be clear here in exposing the tactics of the accuser. Using the woman in Pastor Benny Hinn's story above, let's create a case scenario to show how the accuser would use condemnation to keep a saint out of fellowship with God, prayerless, and away from the church. Once satan has this woman in condemnation, his work is not complete. He then moves his focus to keeping her in condemnation. He is an expert at exposing sin in the saints. After all, Revelation 12:10 says he is the accuser of the brethren. After this woman has had her sinful escapades with adultery, the accuser makes sure it gets back to her church. The saints begin to gossip about her personal life, and she is duly labeled a slut.

One day, this self-condemned saint musters enough faith to arise and go to church. Before the service even begins, she is approached by an immature saint, who says, "I've been hearing bad things about you!" The woman is shocked. Could it be that her worst fears have been realized? Certainly no one at the church knows about her past. The informant continues, "I just couldn't believe my ears when some of the ladies were telling me that you were a home-wrecker. I told them that I knew you and that you have always been a good Christian girl. I know that the things they are saying could not be true. But then they said they had evidence...." Needless to say, the accuser's plan was executed perfectly. Now this woman's condemnation is reinforced by the church. She moves deeper into guilt and separates herself from church for years. Her prayerless life lands her into more sin. All the while, the saints think they are "helping God" by looking down upon her.

In some ministries, the pastor and members police every member's personal life with the intention of making sure that those who sin are put into condemnation. Instead of preaching the power of the blood of Jesus, they preach the wrath of God against His own children. There is a place for preaching the wrath of God in the church, but it is primarily a tool for those who reject Jesus. First Thessalonians 5:9 says, *"For God hath not appointed us to wrath, but to obtain salvation by our Lord Jesus Christ."* Although we may face the discipline of God for our sins, we must clearly understand the lofty position of the children of God. Our future is glorious, and no weakness or sin will change that, because of the blood of Jesus Christ. Romans 5:9 says, *"Much more then, being now justified by His blood, we shall be saved from wrath through Him."* Romans 8:1 also says, *"There is therefore now no condemnation to them that are in Christ Jesus, who walk not after the flesh but after the spirit."*

Often self-condemnation leads to self-flagellation. Self-flagellation is the act of punishing ourselves for sin. It is precipitated by the erroneous thought that God is somehow pleased when He sees us suffer. In a misguided effort to win points with God, many saints will refuse to enjoy simple pleasures of life or fast for extended periods of time. Some may even go so far as giving away their personal possessions, thinking that God will "redeem" them because of their sacrifice. All this they do to show God their contrition. While they think that God is pleased, God is actually grieved.

Hebrews 11:6 says, *"But without faith it is impossible to please God."* The only way we can please God is to believe what He says.

God's Word says, *"If we confess our sins, He is faithful and just to forgive our sins and to cleanse us from all unrighteousness"* (1 John 1:9). God's desire is that we believe His Word and refuse to agree with satan. When we torment ourselves for past sins, it is like telling the devil, "Don't leave. I enjoy having you around." Once and for all, let me set the record straight. God is not interested in punishing the sins of His children. He is interested in delivering His children from their sins, forgiving them, and cleansing them. God not only wants His children free from sin, but He also wants them free from the guilt associated with sin.

The Blood of Jesus

For if the blood of bulls and of goats, and the ashes of an heifer sprinkling the unclean, sanctifieth to the purifying of the flesh: how much more shall the blood of Christ, who through the eternal Spirit offered Himself without spot to God, purge your conscience from dead works to serve the living God? (Hebrews 9:13-14)

Under the Old Covenant, sin was dealt with by the blood of animals. Because Jesus, the Lamb of God, had not yet come to atone for all people's sins, they temporarily offered the blood of animals. The above Scripture makes reference to the old system of atonement through the blood of animals. This Scripture implies that those who offered animal sacrifices under the Old Covenant were forgiven of their sins and that their flesh was purified. Then in contrast, it references the superior blood of Christ Jesus that was offered for our sins. The juxtaposition brings us to one clear conclusion. If they, under the Old Covenant, could receive forgiveness and purification with the blood of an inferior animal, then not only our sins, but even our consciences should be cleansed through our faith in the blood of Jesus.

I did not always understand this reality. For many years I labored under self-condemnation, feeling inadequate before God. My prayer life was very poor because I did not feel God would accept me. But God gave me a revelation of the power of the blood of Jesus, and I was set free from my chains. Yet, I still needed another revelation. Even though I knew I was forgiven eternally, I still wrestled with past sins on a daily basis. God showed me how to daily plead the blood of Jesus over myself and my mind. I had to learn to cast the accuser out of my mind by confessing and believing the blood of Jesus to cleanse my conscience from past sins. Today, when satan tries to bring thoughts of my past to mind, I plead the blood of Jesus over my mind, my conscience, and my heart. My faith in the power of the blood reminds me that I am not only forgiven, but that God has made me righteous by the blood of His Son Jesus Christ.

Endnotes

1. Anton Pavlovich Chekhov, *Note-Book of Anton Chekhov*, trans. S.S. Koteliansky and Leonard Woolf (1921; repr. Middlesex, England: Echo Library, 2006), 81.

2. Benny Hinn, *The Blood* (Lake Mary, FL: Charisma House, 2001), 25-27.

Chapter 5

Group Dynamics

*If the faults we see in other people were not so much
like our own, we would not recognize them so easily.*

—UNKNOWN

Corporate Thinking

THERE IS A sociological principle that asserts that although individuals have their own thoughts and opinions, once they become part of a group, they lose their individuality within the group. They then become a party to the collective mindset of the group they have joined. This is an important concept. This is important because, although most people tend to have their own philosophies, theologies, and ideologies about life, they also belong to other groups and organizations. When people join a church, get a job, join a social club, or even move into a small community, there is an existing "corporate mindset" that is present in the group that the new individuals have joined.

The enemy does not just operate on an individual level; he also operates and manipulates on a corporate level. Let's take the local church as an example. One church may have an evangelistic corporate mentality that focuses on winning lost souls. Another church may have a more closed-minded, "we are the only ones going to heaven" kind of mindset. Because of this, people need to be aware not only of their own personal ideologies, but also of the corporate mindset of the groups they join. People might join a church where, while the enemy does not have control over the individuals, he does exercise influence over the corporate philosophy of the group. Because most people don't study group dynamics, often everyone in the group is spiritually oblivious to the power and influence being exercised over them.

For example, satan can have a dominion of prejudice over an entire church or business that is controlling its corporate actions and destiny. When God seeks to bless that organization through people of another race, they will summarily reject them, yet not consider what they have done as wrong, because it was endorsed by the group. This is why any individual within a church or organization who wants to relay racial stereotypes is a hindrance to that organization. Some businesspeople make the error of allowing certain people within the organization to gossip about and stereotype certain groups. They do this under a banner of "just having fun." What is actually happening is that these evil reporters are destroying the goodwill and unity that makes good businesses great. Employers cannot allow the childishness of gossipers to affect the atmosphere of their business. A godly and professional atmosphere is what God is looking for and what customers and employees are expecting.

The morals and general disposition of a club, sorority, fraternity, church, or community can be satanically controlled by corporate thinking. I have seen entire communities under the spell of corporate control by the enemy. Let us remember that satan does not control the individuals, but because they all buy into a certain group mentality, he is able to exercise great influence over them unawares. Once satan gets them to buy into the group's philosophy, he then raises up men and women within the group who fear to stand for God. He empowers these men and women as the heads of the group. Satan will use people who will not question the group's spiritual disposition.

Often these men and women that satan uses are weak, immature, or carnally-minded Christians who are so distant from their Savior that they do not hear His voice. These types of Christians may become church officers, community leaders, political figures, or social club leaders. Because they confess that they are Christian, we follow them wholeheartedly, but the truth is that satan is well in control. On the other hand, people who will stand up for God are oftentimes ostracized for being too radical or too conservative, or they are criticized because of some imperfection.

> *These words spake his parents, because they feared the Jews: for the Jews had agreed already, that if any man did confess that He was Christ, he should be put out of the synagogue* (John 9:22).

How does this satanic control called "corporate thinking" work? We all desire to be accepted. Every one of us has an inherent need for the approbation and acknowledgment of others. Because the enemy knows this, as soon as he gets control of a group, he brings all who may object to his will under control using the fear of not being accepted. It is called the "fear of exclusion." This type of fear is an intimidating fear, even for mature saints, if they have not made the Lord their prize.

The Bible tells us that *"God has not given us the spirit of fear"* (2 Tim. 1:7). If our lives are being controlled by the fear of being rejected, it is because satan has caused us to buy into his plan to control us. The evidence that we are under this type of controlling influence is that we start to be overly concerned with what everybody else thinks of us instead of what Christ has mandated for us in His Word. When we are under this type of satanic influence, the overwhelming need to be accepted becomes the basis for all of our decisions. Even if Christ would not approve of it, if "everybody else is for it," we feel obligated to accept it. When this unspoken fear begins to control us, we are consumed with the thought, "I need to be accepted." The converse is also true. When there is something that the Lord would have us do, but "everyone else is against it," we feel that same intimidation and zeal for acceptance daunting us.

In this way, satan exercises great control over large groups of people. Working as the accuser, satan uses this "corporate thought" to keep God's spiritual leaders down and out. If God intends to use a certain man to bless His people, the enemy, working within the group mentality, will cause "everybody" to turn against him. When this happens, even mature saints, oblivious to these controlling realities, will conclude, "That's not God's man; everyone is against him." We then enter a series of convoluted circumstances where "everybody" is trying to base their acceptance or rejection of everybody else on what they believe "everybody" thinks.

Here is an example: A pastor leaves a church and there are two top candidates for the open position. The church should pray and ask God for direction, but instead, "group mentality" takes over. Of the two candidates, satan causes the more carnally-minded and political man to be endeared to the people more than the one who is spiritual and godly. Many saints in the group want to speak out about the decision and voice that they think the church is making the wrong choice. But satan quickly whispers in their ears, "Are you really bold enough to go against the whole group? You know you will be rejected." Therefore, the wary saint goes along with the group who votes unanimously on the less spiritual candidate. This decision sends the church into 15 years of fleshly stagnation, but it does not matter, because they all feel "accepted."

The Bible says that, *"God has made us accepted in the beloved"* (Eph. 1:6). Therefore, we need no more acceptance. We would expect that the world would crouch under the pressure of corporate thought, but what a tragedy it is when the Church cares more about being "accepted" by other people than it cares about pleasing the Lord.

People Bondage

Nevertheless, among the chief rulers also many believed on Him but because of the Pharisees they did not confess Him, lest they should be put out of the synagogue: For they loved the praise of men more than the praise of God (John 12:42-43).

Some people live in what is called "people bondage." People bondage is when people cannot separate their personal lives from other people's thoughts and opinions about them. Because they cannot separate the two, they are perpetually governed by the opinions of others. For instance, there is a certain woman I know who keeps her trash in the house because she does not want her neighbors to see what she buys when she goes to the grocery store. That's people bondage! That is, however, a very minor case of people bondage. Another good example of people bondage would be the couple who was engaged to marry, but who broke it off because the people in the community did not think the groom made enough money to marry the daughter of "Dr. Rich Famous." That's people bondage. Different people are controlled at different levels by this sadistic demonic spirit.

I have seen people bondage kill the dreams of many people. A friend of mine wanted to start a business in the town we live in. I was excited about his vision. He is a native of the town, and I shared with him that being a native was an asset to him. Months passed, and there was still no business forthcoming. When I finally saw him, I asked him when he would begin working on the building. His reply was, "Too many people here know me; they won't accept me." I tried to explain to him that the principle of business was meeting needs, not being accepted by people, but he went with people bondage over principle. People bondage is very real in many communities, churches, homes, schools, and businesses. People bondage is the adult form of what we refer to in children and youth as "peer pressure." We often teach our children not to be influenced to do wrong by their peers, while at the same time, we as adults often allow people bondage to control our destiny.

Many saints fear the opinion of other people more than they fear the judgment of God. This is why in many churches there is religious stagnation; the people are not growing in the faith because they have traded away spiritual growth to procure the goodwill of carnally-minded people. What a tragedy it is to see intelligent and conscientious Christian people cower under the influence of people bondage. Once people bondage has set in, gossip becomes a battering ram used to punish those who get out of line with the will of the people. A satanic chokehold then ensues, sapping the life out of God's chosen people. Many churches today are beleaguered by people bondage. The opinions of certain members of the congregation, not the opinions of the Lord, control the destiny of the church. Often these churches are led by pastors too spiritually blind to assess the fact that the church is off course.

Living in Other People's Heads

As a corollary to people bondage, another enemy of progress is noted in the phrase "living in other people's heads." To live in someone else's head means that we are constantly trying to anticipate the opinions of other people. Oftentimes, it is the direct result of having too much exposure to gossip. The prevalence of gossip often makes us paranoid, constantly anticipating what other people will think about us. When we become superconscious of the opinions of other people, we begin to premeditate other people's thoughts about every situation.

For example, the woman who is living in another person's head won't just get up in the morning and get dressed. She has to make the decision on which dress to wear based on what Mrs. Turner is going to think of it. She can't just be herself, because she is bound by the opinions of other people. Other people controlled by people bondage will decide whom they will vote for in political elections based on whom they feel everyone else is voting for. They live in other people's heads. This matter gets even deeper.

When we live in other people's heads and are controlled by people bondage, we will decide not to go to church on Sunday because we are driving a car with a spare tire on it and we don't want anyone to see it. This is the type of control that people bondage has in many Christians' lives today.

There was a certain Christian woman who would fast each Wednesday. One Wednesday she was in the office, and everybody else was going to lunch. They invited her to come along, but she refused. After everyone had left, she began to wonder what the other employees were thinking of her not going to lunch every day. She became overwhelmed with the thought that perhaps they were gossiping about her. Thoughts ran through her head of people saying she was antisocial or arrogant. She broke her fast and rushed down to the cafeteria area to join the others at lunch. When she arrived at the table with her food, they were discussing her, but not the way she thought. Some of the women from the office were dieting, and they were citing her as a good example of a person who was self-disciplined. When she heard this, she was a little embarrassed that she had come.

When we live in other people's heads, we make mistakes by anticipating things that are not factual. A divorced woman who is living in other people's heads may think that every man who does not see her as attractive is rejecting her on the basis of the fact that she is divorced. There may be, however, occasions where our estimation of people's opinions of us are correct, but those people are not worth our basing our lives on their opinions. We must learn to subdue the tendency to try to anticipate what other people think of us or what people are saying about us. Someone once said to me, "Unless you share it with me, it is none of my business what you think of me." This is absolutely true. People's opinions of us are a private matter. We must let other people's thought lives be their own. Being friendly to those who befriend us, we should let other people determine how they would like to relate to us based on their own need for friendship and relationship. Let's stay out of other people's heads.

Gossip as Witchcraft

What begins with one person as evil reporting often escalates to an entirely new, even more pernicious level. At its worst, gossip becomes witchcraft with an extremely satanic and malevolent agenda. Some people may not have come to know gossip in this way, yet the reality is nonetheless true. When people lend their human energy into wishing another person would fail, lose a job, get sick, be exposed, or any other negative thing, what was once gossip has then become witchcraft. This type of spiritual witchcraft can be very effective.

We as human beings have both a human spirit and a natural body. Therefore, we have influence in both the natural and spirit realms. Our spirits and our emotions, even our minds, have some degree of force behind them. When we wish evil on individuals, satan takes that energy and creates an atmosphere of failure for those individuals in the same way that God uses the substance of faith to bless us. This is the same sort of thing that a witchdoctor does. Tragically, it is often us Christians (or those who confess Christ) who are lending their spirits and souls to this type of evil. The Bible says, *"Rebellion is as the sin of witchcraft"* (1 Sam. 15:23). When we wish evil on others, we have "rebelled" against them in allegiance, and we have become a witch to them.

Spiritual witchcraft works especially well in corporate or group settings. The more people lending their spirits negatively toward an individual, the more power the enemy has in creating an environment of failure for that individual. The more human spirits satan has to use against a person, the more effective the witchcraft. I knew of a group of women who had a social club that met once a month. All of the women in the club at once decided they did not like this certain other member of the group because she was different. No one said anything to the woman; neither did they become antisocial with her. They simply all lent their spirits in opposition against her. At the time of the weekly group meetings, this unsuspecting woman was called on to speak, but ironically, she could not get her words out of her mouth. She stuttered in confusion and made simple mistakes in her speech while everyone laughed at her. She could feel the negative energy in the room, but had no idea that the entire group had turned against her. It was not long before her name was erased from the club roll.

We have all seen similar situations. This happens often in churches. Let's just say there is a certain pastor whose services are no longer desired. The congregation can come together in an evil alliance, lending their energies to satan, and thus allowing satan the avenues to attack the unsuspecting pastor. At this point, the pastor's own congregation is now working "witchcraft" on him. This should not be an unusual idea to us as believers; we know from Scripture about the power of the corporate influence of the Church. Whatsoever the Church binds on earth will be bound in Heaven, and whatsoever the Church looses on earth will be loosed in Heaven (see Matt. 18:17-18). Satan can only devour what the Church gives him permission to. When an entire church turns against its pastor, there is a spiritual witchcraft that is released that allows satan a free course to attack that pastor.

This is also one of satan's ways of hindering the Gospel from being preached effectively. Satan will often cause offenses between people as a way of hindering the Gospel. Once there is strife present between individuals, when a person gets up to testify or preach, the animosity and spiritual witchcraft in the room will prevent the unity that precedes the anointing. Psalm 133 tells us that the anointing is preceded by unity. If satan can break the unity, he can preempt powerful preaching. In this way, the Church has often been guilty of practicing witchcraft.

Collateral Damage

Those who participate in evil reporting need not think that the destructive effect of their gossip ends with the person they gossiped with. The truth is, evil reports often have far-reaching consequences that affect the person spoken against long after the conversation is over. Here is a good example. There was a certain prominent doctor who was married and had a large staff of nurses working in his office. The nurses knew the doctor's usual patterns and tendencies. One day an attractive woman who seemed to be quite fond of the doctor came into his office. The doctor saw her as he does many other patients, but in the routine closing session that the doctor spends with the patient explaining her condition and telling her of his prognosis, he spent an unusual amount of time. The nurses knew this was abnormal. Upon subsequent visits, this attractive woman got private time with the doctor. Not long after this, the nurses began to see greeting cards sent to the doctor's office with a hint of perfume. The nurses began to collaborate on the issue. It was not long before the rumor was going around that this doctor was having an affair with one of his patients.

One day, one of the nurses is talking on the phone with a friend of hers about her job. She tells the friend about some of the disappointing and some of the good things about working in the doctor's office. Then, as a good gossip would do, she says, "Girl, guess what...Dr. Thomas is having an affair." The friend replies, "With who...?" The conversation goes on and on about the potential affair this doctor is having. The thing that this nurse does not know is that her telephone friend and this doctor go to the same church. At this church, Dr. Thomas is one of the senior board members. The woman on the phone relays what she has heard from the nurse to her husband, who is also a church official. He then mentions the matter to the pastor. The pastor, knowing the whole matter is only speculation, but not wanting any indiscretion among the leaders of the church, decides to leave Dr. Thomas' name off the list of officers for the upcoming year. Dr. Thomas is angered and disappointed at the pastor's decision, and the two individuals break friendship over the matter. Yet the pastor cannot really discuss his decision, since what he heard was all speculation. Meanwhile, the nurses find out later that the woman who is sending the letters is a longtime friend who has an affinity for sending people greeting cards.

Gossip hurts people far beyond a casual conversation. It separates friends and divides families. Let's take another example. A certain minister and his wife are having serious marital problems. The two just can't seem to get along. The pressures of ministry are extremely demanding, and the wife tends to have somewhat of a temper. One night, the minister comes home late and the wife is steaming angry. When he walks in the door, she starts yelling at him and he starts yelling back. Before they know it, they are hitting each other. A neighbor hears the scuffling and calls the police.

The next day the same neighbor picks up the phone and calls a few friends. The conversation goes like this, "Hey, you know what, that preacher who lives next to me, he came home last night and beat up his wife." Needless to say, everyone who hears it is shocked. The issue gets back to his church and the effects are devastating. He is now uncertain of remaining pastor. Not to mention that people who know of the incident begin to disassociate from him. He and his wife eventually work things out. She begins to pray and to ask God to deal with her anger, and he begins to pray and to ask God to slow him down and give him more time with his family. But the rumor mill has already labeled him an abuser. He leaves the church, but even when he begins to seek another pulpit, the rumor follows him, keeping him for a long time unemployed. If the neighbor would have "prayed" instead of "sprayed," the outcome might have been much better for the pastor.

I would like to share with you one more story that is a good example of collateral damage of gossiping. There is a certain young woman who has a close girlfriend. One night they are confiding in each other. The first young woman tells her friend that she was once in a homosexual relationship. She also shares with her friend some other private matters. Not long after this, this same young woman gets engaged to a young man who is very fond of her. One day he is at church talking with a third young woman who has the eye for him. He tells the young woman that he is engaged and will soon be happily married. When he tells her who his fiancé is, she replies, "Her girlfriend told me she was gay!" The young man wants nothing to do with a "gay" woman, and when he questions his fiancé about it, she tells him that it was something in her past. The two almost break up over the incident.

Evil reporting has collateral damage. It affects people far beyond the initial conversation. When we open our mouths to speak, we must remember that life and death are in the power of the tongue (see Prov. 18:21). We should also remember that the Scriptures say, *"Do unto others as you would have them to do unto you"* (Matt. 7:12). I have found out that the worst nightmare for those who gossip is the thought that someone else may be gossiping about them. If being gossiped about is our worst nightmare, we must ask ourselves why we keep being a nightmare to other people.

Viewing People Properly

My wife once said that "it is easier to 'figure people out' than it is to get to know them." I have found this to be quite true. When we "figure people out," it means that we have found out one or two things about them and have drawn a conclusion about them on the basis of the little we know. We have "figured them out." Getting to know people, however, takes time and effort, not to mention an unbiased approach. Because we tend to lean on "figuring people out," our view of some people gets distorted. The lenses we view people through will determine the color their lives will reflect. We are often guilty of viewing people through lenses of bias and then declaring that their lives are not the color they should be. In actuality, it is our lenses that are the problem. It is so easy to get to the point where we begin to relate to people on the basis of what we may know about them.

For instance, imagine a man is standing on the street corner talking with a friend, and the friend says, "Do you know that guy over there?" referring to another person. The man replies, "Yeah,

I know him. He's the guy who divorced his wife and married his secretary." By doing this, he has created a false relationship to the other man on the basis of gossip. He doesn't really know the man at all. When the friend said, "Do you know him?" the man should have said, "I have seen him before, but I have never formally met him." It is damaging to people to continue to relate to them on the basis of a negative event or experience. Furthermore, we may not know what all was involved in that event.

A person may walk up to another at work and say, "Do you know the woman on the fifth floor who got caught stealing the money?" And for the next 20 years, she then becomes to those people "the woman who stole the money." As Christians, we should renounce stereotyping people and learn to use their names. When we refer to the woman on the fifth floor, we should say, "Mrs. Mary Dunham on the fifth floor is the compliance officer." We should refuse to perpetuate the enemy's accusations against the saints. When we allow Mary Dunham's faults to rest, God will allow our faults to rest.

Nobody's Friend

People who are given to gossip fail to realize they have a sickness. Some people are so inclined to gossip that they place gossip above the dignity of human personality. When their friends and associates realize they are given to gossip, those friends may continue to relate to them socially, but convert into a mode of cautious relations. This is done because they inherently realize that, although they may gossip with their friend about others, they cannot trust that that same friend will not gossip about them. Someone once said that, "If a dog will bring you a bone, he will also carry a bone to someone else." This distrust creates the disintegration of friendships and relationships. Many gossips fail to maintain solid friendships because of their tendency to gossip. They fail to understand that because they gossip about other people, their own friends don't trust them.

Here is an example. Three friends are taking a little excursion to a nearby town. There are two women sitting in the front seat of the car and one woman sitting in the backseat of the car. The friend in the backseat has been gossiping a lot about people in the community. While they are driving, the woman who is in the front passenger seat starts to tell some personal business. Immediately, the woman in the back seat engages the conversation and talks to her all the way to the destination. When the three women get out of the car, the one who was driving pulls the other woman who was sharing her business over to the side and says, "Hey listen, don't tell your business right now, she will go back and tell everybody." After this little evening out, the woman who was sitting in the backseat notices that the other women are not very enthusiastic about inviting her to travel with them anymore, but she has no idea that it has anything to do with gossip. In this way, people who gossip destroy the very fabric of their own relationships because the same people who have gossiped with them don't trust them.

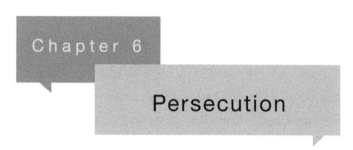

Chapter 6

Persecution

Yea, and all that will live godly in Christ Jesus
shall suffer persecution (2 Timothy 3:12).

IN THIS CHAPTER we will consider the matter of persecution—
more specifically, how the accuser uses persecution to render the
leadership of the Church ineffective. Our Lord Jesus, in a section
of His "inaugural address," better known as the Sermon on the
Mount, had this to say concerning persecution:

> *Blessed are they which are **persecuted** for righteousness*
> *sake: for theirs is the kingdom of heaven. Blessed are ye,*
> *when men shall revile (curse) you, and **persecute** you,*
> *and shall **say** all manner of evil against you falsely, for*
> *My sake. Rejoice, and be exceedingly glad: for great is*
> *your reward in heaven: for so **persecuted** they the proph-*
> *ets which were before you* (Matthew 5:10-12).

According to the *Merriam-Webster* dictionary, the meaning
of the word *persecute* is "to pursue in such a way as to injure or

afflict, to harass, to cause to suffer for one's belief." Although we know that persecution can mean physical assault, it is interesting to note here that Jesus' emphasis is not on physical assault, but on verbal assault. This is because verbal assault is a much more prevalent type of persecution than physical assault. Notice in the above text that Jesus says that believers will be persecuted for righteousness' sake. Then He goes on to say that we are blessed when people revile us. The word *revile* means to abuse verbally or to curse. Then in the same text Jesus says, *"...and say all manner of evil against you falsely."* With these words, Jesus is preparing us for the scourge of the tongue that is often associated with the Christian walk. Let us be very clear in understanding that we will be verbally assaulted for our stand for Jesus Christ, but we as brothers and sisters in Christ need not be a part of the assault on our own family members.

Often, when we think of being persecuted for righteousness' sake, we may feel somehow inadequate. Because we have faults, we may not always feel like we are righteous. Thus, we sometimes misinterpret times when we are being persecuted, assuming that there is no way Jesus could have been referring to us. We should remember that Jesus did not say we would be persecuted "because we are righteous," although we have been made righteous through Jesus Christ. No, the text says that we will be persecuted for *"righteousness' sake."* We are persecuted because we take our stand with righteousness.

This sort of persecution starts even when we are little children. For example, a group of children may decide they will all go down to the corner store and steal some candy. One little boy in the group, however, comes from a Christian home and has been taught by his parents not to steal. At the appointed time, all the children run out of the store with candy in their pockets, but this little boy is too convicted to go along with the group. He decides instead to pay for his candy. What do you think the other kids will do when they find out he did not run out of the store with his candy? Will they applaud him and celebrate him and give him the chief place at the baseball field? Not at all; they will summarily run him down and call him a loser. Why? It is not necessarily because he is righteous, but because he aligned himself with righteousness. Some people, when they get to Heaven, are going to be rewarded for things they did as children that they have long since forgotten.

Each time we align ourselves with righteousness, we are subject to being verbally assaulted. But praise God, Jesus said, *"rejoice...for great is your reward in heaven."* This type of disassociation with the world because of righteousness does not cease after childhood, but goes right on into adulthood. Consider First Peter 4:3, which says:

> *For in time past of our life may suffice us to have wrought the will of the Gentiles* [unsaved], *when we walked in lasciviousness, lust, excess of wine, reveling, banqueting, and abominable idolatries.*

Peter is saying that we did these things when we were unsaved. But the next verse goes on to say, *"Wherein they think it strange that ye run not with them to the same excess of riot, **speaking evil of you**"* (1 Pet. 4:4). Here Peter asserts that the unsaved think we are strange because we are not continuing to go to the same places to commit the same sins of our past. They think it strange that we say "no" to sin and to the world. So what do they do? They speak evil of us. This is the same response the children had in the story I told above. Peter is describing what it is to be persecuted for righteousness' sake. We don't have to be some apostles to be persecuted for righteousness' sake, but simply Christians who make choices for our lives that are in line with God's will.

Let me share an example of persecution that happened in the life of a friend of mine to illustrate how these instances of persecution are everyday experiences. A friend of mine decided she would use her job to the glory of God. She works within a large institution as a support personnel. She works in a position of social services where she has to deal with people who are in trouble financially, socially, or emotionally. As a matter of course, she sees several clients a day. She started using her ministry gift to be an aid and an encouragement to her clients, and she felt like God had uniquely gifted her for the job.

One day, a young man came into her office depressed and discouraged, and she shared with him some things from the Word of God. However, after the young man left her office, he went around telling people she was a religious nut. This young man happened to also be very popular. When other people heard this (as is often the case with gossip—we buy into the negative without reservation), they began to label her the same. Even some of the Christians around the office began to disassociate themselves, acting like they did not want to spend too much time with her. She was being persecuted.

When I told her she was being persecuted by the enemy, she could not get beyond the fact that she did not see herself as holy or worthy to be aligned with those whom Christ referred to as *"persecuted for righteousness' sake."* She simply excused my admonition saying, "Maybe I should have never tried to be helpful. Maybe I should not have tried to be a witness for Jesus." But the opposite was true. She should not have been depressed; she should have been rejoicing. In Matthew 5:12, Jesus tells the persecuted to, *"rejoice and be **exceedingly glad** [ecstatic] for great is your reward in heaven."* Most of the time when these situations occur, instead of rejoicing, the persecuted saint quits the job and the accuser wins. Persecution comes because we align ourselves with righteousness and not necessarily because we are righteousness. The world hates righteousness and wants all people to reject righteousness, as if when this happens God will have to walk away in shame. Even if all people rejected God, He would still be true. Romans 3:4 says, *"Let God be true, but every man a liar...."*

Persecution and Leadership

If there is any one particular group of individuals who get firsthand experience with persecution, it is those who have the call to leadership. Whether we are school principals, politicians, military leaders, businesspeople, pastors, or any other type of leader, we should be apprised of the fact that persecution and leadership often go hand in hand. Because leaders are God's builders, the enemy makes it his business to see to it that there is a constant barrage of criticism and persecution to prevent them from building. Someone once said that the Book of Nehemiah is a manual on leadership. If that is true, it must also be a manual on how to handle persecution. Let us look now at the prophet Nehemiah, who is an excellent biblical model of leadership. He is also to us an example of a persecuted leader and one who endured much evil reporting to finish the work that God called him to do.

Nehemiah

The Book of Nehemiah opens with Nehemiah receiving a report from his fellow Jews of the deplorable conditions of the decimated city of Jerusalem. At the time, Nehemiah and the Jews are in captivity in Babylon, and Nehemiah holds a position of being a cupbearer to the king. It is notable that the Bible tells of no official "calling" from God to Nehemiah, just a personal passion and compassion for the people of God and for the will of God. We should take note of this. How often it is that some Christians are waiting for God to speak to them or give them an official "calling," when God has already given them a passion for that which is His will for their lives. Let us rise up and build for God's unction. It is just as potent as a prophetic word.

Nehemiah was a leader. Leaders cannot sit and watch while things go undone. Leaders are imbued with an urge to change things for the better. Nehemiah starts in the direction of doing something about the breached walls of Jerusalem and finds out God is with him, giving him favor with the king and the people. Whenever we start doing the thing we feel called to do in our hearts, God will confirm His will and His plan for our lives with favor in that particular area. We should note that Nehemiah did not try to rebuild the entire city of Jerusalem. Neither did he seek to rebuild the temple. He only felt a conviction to see the walls of the city rebuilt. One of the biggest mistakes leaders make is to take too much onto themselves. Leaders must remember that they are not called to do everything, but only that which God has graced them to do. Although we may recognize a need for the entire city, we may only be called to a small community. To try to serve outside of our calling brings only frustration and anxiety.

With the king's permission, Nehemiah returns to Jerusalem and views the dilapidated walls. He then sets out to rally the people and initiate the work. The enemy, however, was not very far behind, for we can see his disposition about the matter in Nehemiah 2:10. It reads:

> *When Sanballat the Horonite, and Tobiah the servant, the Ammonite, heard of it, it grieved them exceedingly that there was come a man to seek the welfare of the children of Israel.*

When a true man or woman of God comes forth, satan is not simply grieved, but he is exceedingly grieved. The above Scripture says that these men were grieved because Nehemiah sought *"the welfare of the children of Israel."* The enemy does not just fight any person who claims to be a person of God. The enemy fights the one who has God's people at heart and who desires to do God's will. Nehemiah now becomes the subject of the attack of the enemy because of his sincerity and commitment to God. Ministers and leaders who are sincere will be attacked. Paul warns Timothy, *"Yea, and all that will live godly in Christ shall suffer persecution"* (2 Tim. 3:12).

Nehemiah begins the work of rebuilding the walls and immediately the accuser's pernicious attack begins. We like to think that all wars are of guns and knives, but this war was primarily a war of words. Nehemiah 2:19 says, *"But when Sanballat...and Tobiah...heard it they laughed us to scorn, and despised us, and said, what is this thing that you do...."* The first level of the attack of the enemy is to see if a leader will be abashed by shame or daunted by fear. Some people never make it past this level of attack. They become fearful and intimidated at the fact that some people don't like what they are doing. Therefore, they draw back and fail. What a tragedy it is when we are so spiritually weak that we fall in the grass while others run through high weeds and trees. Many saints have abandoned the will of God because someone called it stupid or despised what was in their hearts.

We see, however, that Nehemiah was not moved by their mockery, but continued to rally the people and build the walls. Nehemiah 4:1 says, *"But it came to pass that when Sanballat heard that we builded the wall, he was wroth, and took great indignation, and mocked the Jews."* We should note here that the text continues to say, *"When Sanballat heard...."* There must have been a lot of gossip surrounding the rebuilding of the walls because Sanballat "hears" everything that Nehemiah is doing. The text also adds that Sanballat had great indignation against Nehemiah. I would imagine that even the Jews back in the Babylonian provinces were saying, "Who does Nehemiah think he is, trying to rebuild those walls?" Sometimes even God's people are too spiritually blind to see what God is doing.

Sometimes we try to act like words don't hurt us, but really they do. Listen to the words of Nehemiah concerning his persecution, *"Hear, O our God; for we are despised: and turn their reproach upon their own head..."* (Neh. 4:4). The scorn, ridicule, and persecution affected Nehemiah, as it does all leaders who are persecuted. Job was another man who came to know the power of the persecutor's tongue. He writes, *"Thou shalt be hid from the scourge of the tongue..."* (Job 5:21). If the tongue did not have a scourge, this would not be necessary to say. Even Isaiah had to petition God for deliverance from the tongue. He declares, *"No weapon that is formed against thee shall prosper; and every tongue that shall rise against thee in judgment thou shalt condemn..."* (Isa. 54:17). The tongue is a very effective weapon, and many people both know it and use it to bring harm to others.

By chapter 6 of the Book of Nehemiah, the accuser is infuriated. He is determined to stop God from having His heritage rebuilt in the land. After a leader has established some momentum and the people have the vision at heart, the enemy usually changes his tactics. No longer using scorn and ridicule, the enemy then seeks to attack the leader directly. The focus ceases to be on group persecution, but turns to a personal attack on the leader. This happens quite often in church settings. Once momentum has been gained for God in a church, satan sets out to discredit the leadership. Sanballat's new strategy was to get Nehemiah distracted. He sent messengers to Nehemiah, saying, *"Come, let us meet together in some one of the villages..."* (Neh. 6:2). But Nehemiah was spiritually astute and knew in his heart that *"they thought to do* [him] *mischief"* (Neh. 6:2). Nehemiah records, *"Yet they sent unto me four times after this sort; and I answered them after the same manner"* (Neh. 6:4). Thank God for focused leadership.

When Sanballat and Tobiah could not distract the leadership, they had one final resort. They began to make false accusations about Nehemiah personally. This is important to the subject of gossip and evil reporting. Godly leadership often has to contend with calumny and gossip. If we are to be effective leaders, we will have to be well-groomed regarding how to deal with modern day Sanballats and the misdirected opinions of people. Nehemiah 6:5-6 says:

> *Then sent Sanballat his servant unto me in like manner the fifth time with an open letter in his hand; wherein was written, "It is reported among the heathen, and Gashmu saith it, that thou and the Jews think to rebel:*

for which cause thou buildest the wall, that thou mayest
be their king, according to these words."

This is a personal attack on leadership. The accuser here seeks to invalidate the integrity of the leader and thereby make the program fail. We know Nehemiah simply wants to rebuild the wall and recover God's city from infamy. However, here comes the accuser saying that he has an ulterior motive of seeking to be king. This is so typical of satan, and we see this type of warfare quite often.

For example, a pastor seeks to align his church with the will of God. His desire is to make changes that will bring glory to God. All of a sudden, he is personally attacked. The enemy begins to attack him through other people over issues of motive, money, or his personal life. All this goes on to keep God's spiritual heritage from being built. Maybe it is a new church building or a youth center or a gymnasium that the pastor seeks to build. It does not matter what he has envisioned; we need to realize that satan does not want God to have a spiritual heritage in the earth. Every time our churches get bigger and more ennobled in the eyes of the community, God is glorified because His people are building His Kingdom in the midst of this satanic world. No wonder there is so much gossip associated with ministry. No wonder pastors are constantly slandered and maligned, and no wonder it is often very difficult to get a building project off the ground. But to God be the glory—the saints are waking up to the schemes of the devil.

I would like to say a final word to pastors and leaders here. Notice carefully that the Book of Nehemiah unfolds with his enemies talking about the project and laughing about it, as if it were unworthy. But by chapter 6, Sanballat sends a letter to Nehemiah saying that it is being *"reported"* that he intends to rebel against Babylon, and this is why he is rebuilding the walls. Now, think with me. Why did that letter have to come to Nehemiah? After all, if Nehemiah is rebuilding the walls to become the king, he knows it. No one needs to tell him of his own motives. Here is a truth. Gossip and evil reporting is effective at turning people against leaders, but gossip is most effective if it gets into the leadership.

I heard a popular preacher say these words, and I believe them to be true: "No matter what people say bad about you, satan will always make sure it gets back to you." The messenger is sent to Nehemiah so that Nehemiah is personally discouraged by the gossip. The accuser wants people to gossip about their pastors or leaders, but satan even more wants the leaders to be discouraged by what they hear is being said about them. People can talk about others every day, but if they do not know it, satan would not be able to discourage them. This is why satan always has a messenger to get the negative words of people back to their leaders. Unfortunately, this messenger is oftentimes the leader's best friend, associate, or family member.

We must remember, as pastors and leaders, that no matter what negative talk is being said about us, satan will always make sure it gets back to us, because what gets back to us affects us. Leaders of all kinds need to guard their spirits and minds against those who are always bringing gossip and evil reports to them— even if they say they are doing it because they are your friends. Pastors and leaders do not need to be constantly bombarded by the talk and opinions of other people. We must learn to leave what the people are saying in the streets so we can hear what God is saying in the closet. **Jesus is the true vine, so let's stop**

listening to the grapevine. All of the evil reporting, all of the gossip, all of the persecution has but one objective—to hinder the work of God.

The Apostle Paul

And it came to pass in Iconium, that they went both together into the synagogue of the Jews, and so spake, that a great multitude both of the Jews and also of the Greeks believed. But the unbelieving Jews stirred up the Gentiles, and made their minds evil affected against the brethren. Long time therefore abode they speaking boldly in the Lord, which gave testimony unto the word of His grace, and granted signs and wonders be done by their hands. But the multitude of the city was divided: and part held with the Jews, and part with the apostles. And when there was an assault made both of the gentiles, and also of the Jews with their rulers, to use them despitefully, and to stone them... (Acts 14:1-5).

We must remember that satan does not have a body; therefore, he employs human bodies to do his work. When he seeks to hinder and destroy, he employs the mouths, hands, and feet of humans to do it. Satanic opposition to ministry is expressed through persecution. We can see this vividly in the life of the apostle Paul. As he went about establishing the churches, he was constantly harassed and persecuted. Everywhere Paul the apostle went, satan stirred up people against him. Acts 14:1 says that Paul preached the Gospel and *"a great multitude both of the Jews and also of the Greeks believed."* Then in verse 2 we read, *"But the unbelieving Jews stirred up the Gentiles, and made their minds evil affected against the brethren."* By the time we get to verse 5, we read that the people have determined to stone Paul. These Jews, telling people evil reports about Paul and the brethren, nearly turned what was about to be a revival into a death sentence.

On another occasion, Paul writes, *"And not rather, (as we be slanderously reported, and as some affirm that we say,) Let us do evil, that good may come? Whose damnation is just"* (Rom. 3:8). Here, Paul is saying that there were people sending out evil reports that Paul and his group intended to do evil. This is the type of thing the accuser depends on to hinder ministry. It is no wonder that Paul constantly requested, *"Pray for me...Pray for us..."* (see 1 Thess. 5:25; 2 Thess. 3:1; Heb. 13:18). He knew the forces that worked against his apostolic ministry. Many Christians watch prayerlessly and aimlessly in churches while certain members trump up charges against the pastor, accuse saints, and cause division—failing to recognize that the accuser is well at work in the midst.

We must remember that persecutors will never acknowledge that they are full of envy, jealousy, resentment, and ill will. They will always make their persecution seem legitimate and justified by making the people they talk about seem like they are immoral, deficient, ignorant, or some other adjective. Persecutors need people to sympathize with the "issue" they raise against the leaders without questioning their motives.

Those who persecuted Paul did not go to the Gentiles and say; "We are evil men who hate Paul for his work for God; would you join with us?" On the contrary, they went to the Gentiles and told them that Paul was the one who was evil and causing trouble. They convinced them that Paul was some sort of an immoral man who sought to do evil. This is the reason the Gentiles got stirred up to stone Paul. The undiscriminating listener will simply hear the report of a persecutor and agree without examination. I have seen people so ill-affected with gossip, so contorted in their thinking by the evil reports of people, that they would not believe the truth even when they heard it. Many saints are so attuned to negative reporting that their senses have become callous to the higher vision of the Church. They are so consumed with petty issues that they will abandon an entire ministry over something as small as a bottle of spilled juice.

The accuser spirit in some places is so strong that it has gotten into the pastors. Instead of them praying for one another, they sit around and talk about one another and one another's ministries. What a tragedy it is when the accuser's work has been so effective that pastors speak evil of each other. Defamation of character is one of the accuser's primary devices for keeping the Kingdom of God offline. Think of what the defamation of a pastor's character does to those who are growing in their faith.

Consider this story. A young unsaved person comes to church and hears the pastor preach. His heart is pricked and he is in the throes of making a decision for Jesus. All the next week he is thinking, *I need to let this world go and choose to walk with God.* He determines to go to church next Sunday and hear the Word preached again. During the week, however, he meets a born-again Christian who is a member of the same church, but who also knows him as a member of the same fraternity. They begin to talk, and the aspiring young convert comments that he enjoyed church on Sunday and that he would definitely be back again. The other Christian man says in response, "Leave your money at home because all the preacher is up there preaching for is money." The next Sunday, the young man is missing from his seat, and things go on as usual. What goes unnoticed is that the accuser has pulled someone once again out of the halls of Heaven, and the angels have to take off their party hats—all because some saint allowed satan to use his tongue.

Jesus says in John 13:35, *"By this shall all men know that ye are My disciples, if ye have love one to another."* The lack of love among Christians is lamentable. The lack of love and respect among pastors and leaders is deplorable. I recently heard of a certain church that had a member who decided to leave and go join a church across town. When the members of the church she had left heard that she had relocated her membership, they were upset. They asked the young woman the reason for her departure. She replied that she was not growing in that church and wanted to be in a church where she would be better taught the Word of God. What do you think was their response? To praise God for her desire to grow in her faith? Not at all. They began a slanderous campaign against the pastor and the church that she had joined, speaking evil of the pastor as an individual and of the church as a group. The young woman who had left the church did not know how to respond to their accusations, so she just stopped going to church altogether.

The Leader's Private Life

We must all realize that the call to leadership and the call to the pastorate does not mean that people cease to have private lives. Although many say they understand this, they oftentimes don't act like they do, especially when it comes to pastors. In Numbers 12:1-2 we read:

And Miriam and Aaron spake against Moses because of the Ethiopian woman whom he had married: for he had married an Ethiopian woman. And they said, "Hath the Lord indeed spoken only by Moses? Hath He not spoken also by us?" And the Lord heard it.

We should first know that it was customary for an Israelite to marry an Israelite. Therefore, for Moses, the leader of the Israelites, to marry an Ethiopian woman was different. However, this was his personal choice. For some strange reason, people have the hardest time understanding that the call of God does not negate an individual's personal uniqueness, interest, or affinities. Therefore, if a woman is called into the ministry and she likes to jet ski, God does not cast jet skiing out of her so that she will be more like others expect her to be. Christians simply have to cast off their religious ways of viewing pastors and leaders. Individual personality and style are not a hindrance, but an asset to ministry. It is "religious" to be intolerant of a leader's idiosyncrasies.

Moses liked a black woman. So what? Get over it! It's his personal choice. But Miriam and Aaron, like many religious people today, chose to *speak* (there's that word again) against the man of God. How often it is that pastors have evil spoken of them because of things in their personal lives that have nothing to do with ministry. "His suits are too expensive." "He needs to buy a new car." "He does not open the door for his wife." "She dresses too fancy to be a pastor." Being church members does not give us the legal right to deride or judge the leaders for their personal choices. Their personal lives are between them and God. Let's stay in our lane, keep our mouths in check, and allow God to do the rest.

I want to take another look at the Scripture above. We should note that Miriam and Aaron took their assessment of an error in Moses' personal life as an opportunity and justification for undermining his spiritual authority. In verse 2 they say, *"Has the Lord indeed spoken only by Moses? Hath He not spoken also by us?"* This is an interesting and important point. They saw something objectionable in Moses' personal life and then decided that Moses should no longer be able to exercise spiritual authority. How many times have we seen an officer in the church wrest power and authority from the pastor as a result of something about the pastor's personal life he objected to.

For instance, a pastor gets a divorce, and the officers then declare, "Has God spoken only by him? Has He not spoken by us also?" With this evil report, they begin a campaign to steal spiritual authority from the man of God. But God is displeased with their arrogance. Verse 4 of the text reads, *"And the Lord spake suddenly unto Moses and unto Aaron, and unto Miriam, 'Come out ye three...'"* (Num. 12:4). The Lord then addresses Aaron and Miriam, saying:

> *My servant Moses is not so, who is faithful in all Mine house. With him will I speak mouth to mouth, even apparently, and not in dark speeches...**wherefore then were ye not afraid to speak against** [him]?* (Numbers 12:7-8).

That's a good question. If God has ordained particular people of God for the work, why are there so many gossips in the church who are not afraid to speak against them? Miriam and Aaron are like so many in the church who have failed to discern the need to cease from gossiping. We would do well to learn what God says in Psalm 105:15, *"Touch not Mine anointed, and do My prophets no harm."* What was the end of the matter with Miriam and Aaron? Did God say, "Well since you only gossiped against Moses, I am going to let you off the hook"? Not so. Verse 9 says,

And the anger of the Lord was kindled against them; and He departed. And the cloud departed from off the tabernacle; and behold Miriam became leprous, white as snow: and Aaron looked upon Miriam and behold, she was leprous (Numbers 12:9-10).

Notice the punishment was threefold. First, the text says that the Lord departed. This is the first punishment for speaking against God's leaders. Many churches don't realize that the absence of the Lord's presence is a direct result of gossip and persecution against leaders in the church. Second, the cloud departed. This indicates a loss of spiritual direction and purpose. Third, Miriam became leprous. The only reason Aaron did not become leprous was because he was the high priest. Leprosy would have prevented him from serving as such. Leprosy is a degenerative skin disease. It represents a type of the spiritual cancer that sets in when a church has allowed gossip, slander, and evil-speaking to go on.

There is a "leprosy" on many churches today that will not be lifted until the people ask their leaders to forgive them for the maliciousness of their words. Leadership in any organization must take note of their speech also, so as to never speak evil of their members and bring a hindrance upon their own work. Leaders must also remember to never speak negative words about other leaders. Our candles do not shine any brighter by blowing someone else's candle out.

Chapter 7

Judging

People's natural inclination [is] to be easy on themselves, judging themselves according to their good intentions— while holding others to a higher standard and judging them by their worst actions.

—JOHN C. MAXWELL[1]

Judge not, that ye be not judged. For with what judgment ye judge, ye shall be judged: and with what measure ye mete, it shall be measured to you again. And why beholdest thou the mote that is in thy brothers eye, but considerest not the beam that is in thine own eye? Or how wilt thou say to thy brother, "Let me pull the mote out of thine eye"; and behold, a beam is in thine own eye? Thou hypocrite! First cast the beam out of thine own eye; and then thou shalt see clearly to cast out the mote out of thy brother's eye (Matthew 7:1-5).

There is much we need to learn about judging. A dictionary definition of the word *judge* is:

1. To form an authoritative opinion. 2. To decide as a judge: to try. 3. To form an estimate or evaluation about something. 4. To give an opinion.[2]

There is a positive aspect of judging that we often refer to as "ruling." In a baseball game, an umpire "judges" or "rules." But the type of judging we will discuss here is more a type of presumptive, negative, and condescending disdain that one person has toward another person who has a fault or who is at fault.

The Bible does speak of instances where we must "rule" in terms of what would be a hindrance to the church or to our faith. Paul writes in Romans 16:17, *"Mark them which cause divisions and offenses contrary to the doctrine which ye have learned; and avoid them."* Paul here warned the Roman Christians to guard their faith by judging those among them who did not believe the true Christian doctrine. There are instances in life where we have to "rule," and there are many examples of this in Scripture. There is also a negative type of judging, the type that the Bible always condemns. This type of judging is when we make personal estimations of people based on their faults or on what we may know about their personal lives.[3]

In the text from Matthew, Jesus begins simply and accurately. He says, *"Judge not, that ye be not judged..."* (Matt. 7:1). His opening words affirm that people who judge their brothers and sisters are immediately on the judgment seat themselves. To venture to make a personal condemnation of other people's faults is to say, in effect, "OK, God, I am ready to be judged." The above text does not identify the second "judge" who judges the first person, who is presumptuously judging another. We might presume it is God who will judge. However, I believe judging our brothers and sisters puts us in the light of the judgment of both God and other people.

One of the things I always like to point out about the above text is the fact that Jesus acknowledges that the man being judged has a mote in his eye. People often feel like they need to judge others because they have actually recognized some faults, sins, or impediments in the lives of the people they are judging. They feel as if their judgment would be improper if they did not know that what they were judging the person about was true. But in the above text, Jesus does not disallow the fact that the brother has a mote in his eye. This mote represents a fault or a sin.

Jesus also implies through the text that He does want him to get delivered from the mote. The only problem is that the one who desires to get the mote out of his brother's eye is more in need of the mercy and forgiveness of God than the one who has the mote. Jesus says concerning the one who is doing the judging that he has a beam (a log) in his eye. This simply means that being judgmental is a greater sin than any personal fault of an individual. I have heard many Christians say, "There is no such thing as big sins and little sins." But Jesus said on another occasion, *"Thou couldest have no power at all against me, except it were given thee from above: therefore he that delivered me unto thee hath the greater sin"* (John 19:11). Logs are bigger and more sinful than motes, and judging is a greater fault than any personal sin. Jesus wants us free from the need to judge one another even more than He wants us delivered from personal weaknesses.

There is one more thing I would like to point out here. Often, when Christians are judging others, they will say that the

Christians who have sin in their lives are hypocrites. This is what I have heard all my life. If some other Christians were doing something they should not be doing, and the saints found out about it, they would say that that those Christians were hypocrites. But notice in the above passage who the hypocrite is. Jesus speaks to the man who is judging his brother for his sin (mote) and says, *"Why beholdest thou the mote that is in thy brother's eye but considerest not the beam that is in thine own eye...**Thou hypocrite...**"* (Matt. 7:3-5). Jesus calls the person who is doing the judging the hypocrite. I wonder how many hypocrites we have in the Church who are running around calling other people hypocrites because of their personal faults.

God is trying to teach us to be patient and forbearing, forgiving and loving toward one another as He is toward us. Here is a powerful conclusion to this truth about judging: the degree to which we hold the faults of other people against them, is the degree to which God will hold our faults against us. As we explore this matter of evil reporting, let's examine whether we have spoken evil of our brothers and sisters with the intention of holding their sins against them. If and when we do this, God is holding our sins against us. Paul writes in Romans 2:1:

> *Therefore, thou art inexcusable, O man, whosoever thou art that judgest: for wherein thou judgest another, thou condemnest thyself; for thou that judgest doest the same things.*

Another vivid biblical example of someone who had to be delivered from the spirit of judgment was Ananias. The Book of Acts chapter 9 records the conversion of Saul of Tarsus, whom we later come to know as the apostle Paul. Saul saw a great light on his way to Damascus. It was the white light of Christ that was efficacious in saving his soul. When Jesus was finished with Saul on the Damascus road, he was blind and confused, but aware that he had met the Lord. In preparation for Saul's entering into the Christian Church, God called Ananias, a godly man, who would lay hands on Saul so that he would recover his sight. The Lord spoke to Ananias and said, *"Arise and go into the street which is called Straight, and enquire in the house of Judas for one called Saul of Tarsus; for behold, he prayeth"* (Acts 9:11). What was Ananias' reaction when he heard that it was Saul of Tarsus whom the Lord was sending him to? In verse 13 Ananias says to the Lord, *"Lord, I have heard by many of this man how much evil he hath done to Thy saints at Jerusalem"* (Acts 9:13).

Because of what Ananias had "heard," he was hindered in his obedience to the Lord. Many saints today are hindered in some way or another by what they have heard. Ananias clung to the reports of the people about Saul. Then the Lord encouraged Ananias and also gave Saul a commendation, *"Go thy way [Ananias], for he is a chosen vessel unto Me to bear My name before the Gentiles, and kings, and the children of Israel"* (Acts 9:15). Now it is only fitting that Ananias would fear Saul based on what he had heard, but what is so ironic is that Ananias thinks the Lord is trying to set him up to be killed. The Lord would not do that. Although it is understandable in the case under consideration, we must also consider how clinging to the opinions of people can affect the work and calling of men and women of God. God often uses people who do not have impeccable pasts.

Let's say a certain man has been to prison. When God commissions him to go forward and be a witness, many saints get caught up in analyzing the things he did that sent him to prison.

When they hear that this same man is preaching the Gospel in a powerful way, they may declare, "I have heard many things of this man." Because of gossip, they may be inhibited from receiving him as a vessel of God. God may then tell a certain saint to get up and go help this man's ministry. This saint may then sit and think to him or herself, "I think I hear the Lord telling me to go join that man's ministry, but I have heard many things about what he did in his past and how he went to prison." Because of our insensitivity to the leading of the Holy Ghost, we make our own decisions, all the while singing, "Where He leads me, I will follow...."

I would even venture to say that if it were not for a direct manifestation of the Lord to Ananias, Saul would have been blind for a long time. For many years, Paul was in infamy among the disciples. Acts 9:26 says, *"And when Saul was come to Jerusalem, he assayed to join himself to the disciples: but they were all afraid of him, and believed not that he was a disciple."* There are those among us whom the saints "believe not" that they are of God because of all the gossip. However, if we can get beyond their mistakes, we will be able to see both the mercy of God and the glory of God.

Years later, Paul wrote, *"Being confident in this very thing, that He which hath begun a good work in you will perform it until the day of Jesus Christ"* (Phil. 1:6). Since the day I gave my life to Jesus Christ, God has been performing a work of grace in me. I have found that a believer does not necessarily get saved and sanctified on the same day. Once we are born again, we are saved from wrath. However, getting delivered from sin is a process; we often refer to it as sanctification. When I was born again, I was delivered from some sins immediately. Other weaknesses continued to harass me years after my salvation experience. I had to learn to lean on God's grace for victory in some areas.

However, my weaknesses did not prevent my calling into the ministry nor my commissioning as a pastor, which God did according to His divine will. I can remember times in my life when I had struggles with sin. But what is interesting is that even when I failed, God never stopped teaching me. I was never separated from the love of Jesus. I can remember a time in my life when I was under serious attack from the enemy. My personal faults and decisions had given satan a door of opportunity to destroy me. One day, while all alone, I came under an attack from the enemy, and I started having a heart attack. This was an unusual heart attack. I could literally feel the tentacles of something demonic gripping my heart, trying to kill me. I had to call on the name of Jesus.

How did a demon do that to me if I am a child of God? Everything in the spirit realm works on legal grounds. Satan wants to destroy all saints, but he cannot. He spends his time *"seeking whom he may devour"* (1 Pet. 5:8). Often, sin in the life of a believer can be a doorway to attack from the enemy. We are in spiritual warfare. In a natural war, if a soldier casually walks out from behind his cover, he may receive some steel "air mail," or bullets. Likewise, a saint living in sin is like a soldier walking openly across a battlefield in the midst of war. Maturity and growth in the Christian life are extremely important. While some may see the Christian life as a blissful oasis of glory, in truth, it is warfare.

After the heart attack episode, I was watchful and prayerful for another physical assault from the enemy. But satan is wise, and he changed his tactics on me. Formerly under physical attack, I then began to come under great mental warfare. I started to feel like I was going to lose my mind. Day and night I started having thoughts that I did not know where I was going or what I was doing. I did not know what was going to happen to me next. I started to fear for the worst. Satan was taking advantage of me through the doorway of sin in my life. But thanks be to God! He brought me through, delivered me from sin, and restored my mind. Saints, we must take the enemy seriously and not think lightly of the presence of sin in our lives.

Now why did I share all of that? Because all the while I was going through that experience, I was being judged by my brothers and sisters in Christ for the fault in my life. The thing I found ironic was that a year later I was approached by a young woman who was in the same situation. Because of her personal choices, satan had found an avenue to attack her mentally. She felt like she was losing her mind, and she was in the throes of fear, doubt, and anxiety. She told me she needed help badly. I was able to minister to her out of my own brokenness in that area, and help her get her deliverance.

Here is my point. No matter what we go through, God is committed to transforming us into the image of His dear Son, Jesus. Our failures often become our greatest source of ministry anointing. This is why we should not judge one another for faults. God has a tendency to use people who have had a weakness or two. Often divorcees become the greatest teachers on the importance of marriage. Often former drug addicts become the greatest source of inspiration for those dealing with addiction. On and on we may go. The point is that whatever we have struggled with is the thing we should minister to someone else about.

We must not spend our time judging those who are down with a fault right now, but instead pray for them and praise God in advance for the testimony and ministry that will come out of it. A Christian singer wrote his autobiography, and in it he talked about how he had association with homosexuality. Later in his life, he wrote a popular song that says, "We fall down, but we get up...." If this believer could fall down and get back up again, so can our neighbors, our children, our church members, and even our pastors. The spirit of judgment is holding saints down; let's allow them to get back up.

> *Brethren, if a man be overtaken in a fault, ye which are spiritual, restore such a one in the spirit of meekness; considering thyself, lest thou also be tempted* (Galatians 6:1).

Galatians 6:1 describes what is called the ministry of restoration. The Church today is desperately in need of a resurgence of this important ministry. It is a ministry that the spiritually mature of the Church are to administrate. I have found very few churches that take this Scripture seriously enough to begin training people for this work. Sometimes it even seems that we would rather talk about the saints than restore the saints. In many churches, they sing the song, "I'm on the battlefield for my Lord...." I am glad the saints are out there fighting, but God help us if we get wounded by sin. There is very little chance of our recovery.

Those who are spiritual, whom the Holy Spirit is calling to the ministry of restoration, should get to work. There are a lot of wounded soldiers on this Christian battlefield who are in need of restoration. It is important to note that Galatians 6:1 does not say, "If a man has a fault." The reference here is toward people who are *"overtaken in a fault."* This means that they have started to wear their sins. Their issues are affecting themselves, their families, and other people. Upon these people the Church must act.

God says we are to commission those who are truly spiritual to counsel these brothers and sisters in Christ.

But when they are sent, they are to go "considering themselves." This simply means that those sent to counsel people who are overtaken in sin might have the tendency to fall into the sin of pride and being judgmental. In doing the work of restoration, there can easily arise an attitude of "Why are you so stupid to keep doing the things you are doing?" If this type of pride sets in, the restoring saints then have "logs" of judgment in their eyes and have thus become hypocrites in need of restoration themselves. We have preached that the Church has the power to heal the sick, raise the dead, and cast out demons. Our greatest challenge, however, still lies before us. That challenge is: Can the Church heal the sinner?

The Spirit of Judgment and Marriage

One of the areas where we must be aware of the work of the accuser is in marriage. There is absolutely no limit to the destruction that the accuser can cause to a marriage through the spirit of criticism and judging. Controlling the tongue needs to be a continual aim for every husband and wife because everything that is said in a marriage either helps or hinders, heals or scars, builds up or tears down the marriage. Once we notice something about our spouses' character that we do not admire, it is important that we consider ourselves, lest we also are tempted (see Gal. 6:1). Otherwise, the accuser will quickly step in to bring in the spirit of judgment and criticism about the fault we have noticed.

For instance, a wife gives a certain responsibility to her husband. She is depending on him to do some things that she considers very important, and seemingly each time she depends on him, he fails to come through. He does not appear to understand the negative impact this omission has. She becomes angry, even bitter about it. The thoughts in her head are, *He is so stupid; he can't even complete one simple task.* The accuser then begins his work of sowing division in her heart. If she does not repent of her critical spirit, the accuser will be able to put the marriage on the line by causing her to feel that divorce is the only answer. Because she indulges in being critical toward him, she is not able to appreciate the good things that he does do daily toward her. She is too overtaken by those things he failed to do.

It is important to remember that when we marry, we do not marry a person who is just like we are. Our spouses do not have the same temperament, inclinations, strengths, or even weakness as we do. Therefore, what may be important to one spouse often is not as important to the other. Thus, we must be mindful of our differences. In the above case, instead of judging and criticizing, the wife should adjust herself. She should give less responsibility to her husband in some areas, while capitalizing on the things he does do well and the things he does get done. She must also remember her own imperfections. If she begins to speak against her husband to friends or family, she empowers the enemy, because she aligns herself with the accuser against her husband. The accuser then begins to use her testimony to cause her to destroy the marriage with her own mouth.

Another example might be a husband with a wife who has a tendency to talk too much. The accuser is on his job, causing the husband to resent and judge his wife. Satan causes him to feel as if he would love to have a wife who would just be quiet sometimes. This leads him into discontentment with his marriage. He begins to cease to appreciate his wife's commitment and dedication to the home because he has judged her for being garrulous. The enemy is busy working in his heart and, if possible, in his mouth. The husband may begin to speak to other people about how he is dissatisfied with his wife, criticizing her for being too opinionated. The enemy's work then is to send another woman his way who seems quiet and unassuming. When he meets this woman, the enemy will begin to tell him that he married the wrong person. Because he did not repent of his judgmental attitude toward his wife, he has placed his marriage in jeopardy.

"Accurate Judgment" vs. "Right Judgment"

Oftentimes, we may feel legitimate in judging our spouses because we feel we have firsthand information about them, and we feel we have judged accurately. We feel like we know them and have made a proper assessment of them, and therefore are justified in our conclusion. But what we call "righteous" judgment is actually "accurate" judgment. Accurate judgment is based on the information we have. For instance, I am a former mathematics teacher. If I have an equation with three variables, and I have knowledge of the value of two of the variables, I can solve the equation to a certain point, but the ultimate conclusion I cannot reach because I don't have the last variable.

In the same way, we may have some of the facts about our spouses. We know their outward actions and their proclivities, but we do not really know their hearts, or all of their past experiences, or their weaknesses, or their good intentions. We are powerless to assess what things our spouses would like to change about themselves but cannot. A wife may know her husband needs to stop drinking, but she cannot also tell how in his heart he desires to change and has tried many times and failed. A husband may know that his wife is mean to him, but cannot conclude that she merely wants the best for him and has never been taught how to effectively relate to a man. "Accurate" judgment does not mean "right" judgment.

The apostle Paul addressed this issue of accurate judgment versus right judgment when he wrote to the church at Corinth. They had judged him as an apostle and, by some criteria, concluded he was inadequate. In First Corinthians 4:3-5, he says:

> *But with me it is a very small thing that I should be judged of you, or of man's judgment: yea, I judge not mine own self. For I know nothing of myself; yet am I not hereby justified: but He that judgeth me is the Lord. Therefore, judge nothing before the time, until the Lord come, who both will bring to light the hidden things of darkness, and will make manifest the counsels of the hearts: and then shall every man have praise of God.*

Paul informs us that when Christ shall judge, He will judge not only by actions, but also by the counsels of the heart. This we cannot do. At the judgment seat of Christ, many who have done good things will be found to have done them for the wrong reasons. Similarly, in that judgment, many who have not been perfect will be exposed as having had good intentions. Let those of us who are married not judge our spouses, for the Lord shall judge at the appointed time. Brothers and sisters, *"let us love one another: for love is of God"* (1 John 4:7). As we mature in our walks with God and in our marriages, we will learn to love our spouses and embrace their weaknesses as well as their strengths. God never promised us perfection in marriage; that was our idea. But now that we have come back down to earth, let's get busy learning how to live with people who are just like we are—imperfect.

Contempt Toward Our Spouses

Let us press forward a little further with this matter of judging in marriage. We have talked briefly about not judging our spouses for outward acts and inadequacies. Now I want to expose the accuser on a deeper level in dealing with those who may have contempt toward their spouses in their hearts. Contempt is a deeper type of judgment. The *Merriam-Webster* dictionary definition for *contempt* is "to despise or to hold in disrespect."[4]

An example of this might be a couple that is happily married, but the wife perceives her husband to be arrogant. She feels that ever since he got that certain job, he thinks he is more important than everyone else. On the surface of the marriage, everything seems fine, but in her heart, he is despised. She privately wishes he would lose the new job. Her judgment of him will not go unnoticed by the accuser. He uses it to draw a wedge between the two of them. To everything this husband does, the accuser whispers in the wife's ear, "Don't respond; don't assist him. He's only doing that to show off." With this judgment, the enemy is given ammunition to weaken the marriage.

What the wife should actually do is wait. If her husband is arrogant, God will humble him in due time. She should keep on loving her husband even with his imperfections. Through her humility, God can show her husband he has the wrong attitude. So often I have found in these situations that a wife may hold her husband in contempt for being arrogant, but upon talking with the husband, he says something like, "All my life I wanted to be somebody. My father was never accomplished, and I felt like I might have the same fate. My job is all I have in terms of self-esteem. I just wanted my wife to be proud of me. That is why I try so hard." What the wife was holding him in contempt over was really caused by good intentions. That is why the Scriptures say, *"Judge nothing before the time..."* (1 Cor. 4:5).

Another example of contempt might be in regard to things our spouses cannot change about themselves. Often after marriage, the enemy will look for a place in the heart of a spouse to sow jealousy or contempt. He may cause a husband to be jealous over his wife's job, education, or friends. He may seek to cause a wife to be jealous over her husband's talents or material success. Any of these situations may apply to your own marriage. The accuser is at work sometimes even in matters as abstract as causing a husband to have contempt for his wife because she has been previously married, or vice versa. The issue of parity in relationships may become a big problem when only one spouse has been previously married. Often, when one person meets another and they fall in love, they may be able initially to overlook the fact that one person was previously married. However, I have learned that while it may be initially negligible, the lack of marital status parity can come back to haunt a relationship.

Often, when people marry previously divorced people, they may initially feel only love. Later, as the marriage progresses, they may feel judgment and contempt for the previously married spouse. These people then may feel as if they "settled for less" since their spouses were previously married. If those individuals are not spiritually mature, they may feel that they have the right to judge their previously married spouses, and may seek a divorce as a solution to the dilemma. Instead of clinging to their marriage, they throw it away in judgment of their spouse. Of course, once those spouses divorce, they are then both divorcees, and the cycle is restarted. On a cool July evening, a certain husband makes a certain mistake, and the wife says, "You should know by now how to treat a woman," or "You didn't learn this in your first marriage!" The state of her heart is that she holds contempt toward him for having been previously married. She has thus judged her husband for how his life has unfolded and for decisions and circumstances of his past.

I have met people who held their spouses in contempt because they did not get what they wanted in a spouse. A certain woman may have always dreamed of a tall, dark, and handsome man, but never found him. A certain man may have always dreamed of marrying someone who looks like a supermodel, but his supermodel of a wife now weighs 300 pounds. The enemy attaches himself to these negative thoughts and uses them to weaken these marriages. Who said life was about finding the "perfect spouse"? The Church today is too worldly, and we often, like the world, get too involved with trying to find spouses who will validate us and make us feel significant. Men seek an attractive wife, and women may seek an attractive man in order to affirm their own need for self-esteem.

However, life is not about self-esteem, but about finishing our course. When all is said and done, the real question of life will be, did we finish our course? Did we fulfill God's will for our lives? John the Baptist was never married, but the Bible says in Acts 13:25 that he finished his course. Did he get the perfect spouse? No, he didn't get one at all. But he did the will of God in his life. Paul the apostle was never married, but I don't remember him complaining about it in any of his letters. Instead, in Second

Timothy 4:7 we hear him say, *"I have fought a good fight, I have finished my course, I have kept the faith."* Life is not about marrying attractive spouses, but about fulfilling God's will for our lives. Those of us who are married must be ever so watchful of the accuser. Let us be quick to be gracious and quick to forgive. Give no place to the devil.

Family: I Can't See Any Good in You!

So far I have elaborated on the matter of judging and how having a critical spirit affects our view of others. At its worst, a judgmental spirit is blinding. It prohibits us from seeing the good in other people. This is most evidently true within families. Sometimes sisters and brothers or children and parents can become so critical of one another that they stop being able to see the good in each other.

For example, there are two older men I know who are brothers. They are both my friends and are both great people. I think the world of each of them. But they don't think well of one another. They are highly critical of each other and have been for years. Although they both love God and they both do a lot of good for other people, they still fail to see any good in one another. Often, when I visit with them, I will talk to them individually. I will sit and talk to the first man, and he will say, "My brother down the road is the sorriest man on the planet. All he does is sit around all day and read the Bible. He don't even clean up his house." After I finish visiting with this brother, I will walk down the road to the other brother's house. We will talk awhile, then he will say, "Did you stop by my brother's house up the road?" "Yes," I will reply. He then will say, "There ain't no good in that man. All he does is drink his beer. He should not be an elder in the church at all." In this way, the enemy perpetuates division and strife.

This is often the case in families as well as in marriages. A husband and wife can both become so critical of one another that they stop seeing the good. Blinded by the accuser, they begin to feel that divorce is the only answer. The fallacy in all of this is the false assumption that "my spouse is supposed to be perfect, but isn't." The judgmental spirit, backed by the accuser, destroys marriages, families, and friendships.

Judging and Rulers

Submitting yourselves to every ordinance of man for the Lord's sake: whether it be to the king, as supreme; or unto governors, as unto them that are sent by Him for the punishment of evildoers, and for the praise of them that do well. For so is the will of God, that with well doing ye may put to silence the ignorance of foolish men (1 Peter 2:13-15).

Here is a passage of Scripture many Americans need to study well. The Lord is instructing us through the apostle Peter about our witness in this world toward our government. He begins by saying that we must "submit ourselves" to every governmental ordinance for the Lord's sake. This means that, since we are God's representatives in this world, for the sake of our witness, we should have a positive attitude toward our government. This text outlines who we should be in submission to. It mentions first and foremost *"the king, as supreme."* The reason it says "as supreme" is because it is referring to a principle. We should be in submission to whoever is the highest authority in the land we live in. Then this passage informs us that we should also be in submission to lesser authorities, calling them "governors."

We as Christians should make sure we have a good witness in the earth by being in submission to earthly authorities. This brings glory to our God as we live in this rebellious world. This is why the last part of the verse says, *"that with well doing you may put to silence the ignorance of foolish men"* (1 Pet. 2:15). People who do not abide by the law and people who do not respect their government should feel stupid when they are around Christians because of the submissive and obedient spirit we have toward authority. However, some Christians have a very poor witness when it comes to the area of submission to authority. God is a God of authority. No matter how much we may not like being under authority, our rebellion will be to our own peril if we are not under authority in the home, on the job, in our schools, in government, and in the Church. God works through authority.

> *Let every soul be subject unto the higher powers. For there is no power but of God: the powers that be are ordained of God. Whosoever therefore resisteth the power, resisteth the ordinance of God: and they that resisteth shall receive to themselves damnation (judgment). For rulers are not a terror to good works, but to the evil. Wilt thou then not be afraid of the power? Do that which is good and thou shalt have praise of the same. For he is the minister of God to thee for good. But if thou do that which is evil, be afraid; for he beareth not the sword in vain: for he is the minister of God, a revenger to execute wrath upon him that doeth evil* (Romans 13:1-4).

We must learn as Christians to praise God for godly leadership. For instance, I don't consider myself to be Republican or Democrat. I vote according to Christian principles. This means that I search to see which candidate is the most in accord with biblical values; then I vote accordingly. Christians should vote God's will, and not according to popularity polls or political affiliation. So many saints are immature or unlearned and vote based on which candidate they believe will "throw them a bone." The Bible says that God has *"cattle on a thousand hills"* (Ps. 50:10). Likewise, He has money in a thousand banks, and blessings in a thousand vaults.

I have met people who live in America and absolutely despise the president of our country. This, of course, is their inalienable right. They have the right to express their opinion just as I do. But what is more than the expression of our opinions is sin. I have heard many people ignorantly rail on and on about how they hate a certain president, how they think he's stupid, and how we would not have had war, inflation, or high gas prices if that president had not been in office. It seems that freedom of speech has caused many Americans to lose their sense of responsibility to bless the king as supreme. God raises up people to sit on the throne and to govern the people. For this reason, the witness of believers ought be according to Exodus 22:28, *"Thou shalt not... curse the ruler of thy people."*

The toxic mouths of many American Christians have been more pernicious than those of some foreigners against the men and women who lead our nation. It is not an honorable thing for a citizen of this country to speak evil of America or of the president. There are some people who perpetually curse the country and its leadership. They never have a positive word to say about any president. They bring great condemnation upon themselves, never realizing that they and God are not in accord. If they would speak a blessing, they would receive a blessing. Because these people have chosen to speak a curse on their president, they have forfeited certain favor from God. We must bless America and speak well of our country. And we must not associate with those who will speak curses on this nation.

I talk with many foreigners in my line of work. When they first come to this country, for many of them, the most striking thing they notice about America is the large numbers of Christian churches they see. They also note how many signs, bumper stickers, and billboards they see that promote Jesus Christ. They know immediately that they are in a Christian nation. While people coming from outside our country can see the Christian influence, many within this nation have focused so hard on America's faults that they have given up on this nation. Some Christians feel like they are justified in degrading America because they see its imperfections. They see moral, social and political corruption, and they think they are called to deride the nation.

I too am concerned about some of the moral decadence in this nation, but God did not tell me to add more decay to our country by offering my toxic tongue. I am to promote Jesus Christ, who will subdue all things to Himself. We as Christians should not be looking for judgment to come upon America; we should be praying for and expecting revival. It is not our place or authority to rebuke presidents; that is God's job. People who feel they can rebuke presidents simply don't know their rank. By saying this, I do not mean that a president should be allowed to break the law. I mean that if a president's agenda does not line up with our expectations, it is not our place to malign, slander, whisper, or gossip against him. He is the president.

Paul employed this principle when standing before judgment in Acts 23:1-5. They brought Paul in before a group of men, one of whom was the ruling high priest, Ananias. Paul was unaware that he was standing before the high priest. As Paul gave his deposition to the group, Ananias commanded one of the soldiers to smite Paul on the mouth. In anger Paul responded, saying to Ananias, *"God shall smite thee, thou whited wall: for sittest thou to judge me after the law, and commandest me to be smitten contrary to the law?"* (Acts 23:3). When Paul said this, those who stood by said, *"Revilest thou God's high priest?"* (Acts 23:4). Paul's response was, *"I [knew] not, brethren, that he was the high priest: for it is written, 'Thou shalt not speak evil of the ruler of thy people'"* (Acts 23:5). We should take note that Paul could say this even though the high priest had just had him unjustly slapped by a soldier. Finding a fault in leaders does not give us the right to speak evil of them or judge them. God does not need us to tell Him what is wrong with a president or other leader. We should not speak evil of our president, governor, mayor, council member, or any other leader of our people.

The Bible also refers to pastors as rulers. Hebrews 13:7 is referring to pastors when it says, *"Remember them which have the rule over you, who have spoken unto you the word of God: whose faith follow, considering the end of their conversation."* Hebrews 13:17 continues in the same vein, saying:

> *Obey them that have the rule over you, and submit yourselves: for they watch for your souls, as they that must give an account, that they may do it with joy, and not with grief: for that is unprofitable to you.*

We should consider our pastors to be rulers under God. Because of this, we should not speak evil of them for their work. They are judged of God, who needs no assistance. Whether we know it or not, God is not clueless. He even knows our thoughts from afar (see Ps. 94:11). God is well able to rebuke whoever needs it. Let us therefore speak blessing and not curses upon our churches and leaders. Many saints have nothing positive to say about their leadership. Their every word is decrying some imperfection in the church. And by doing so, they prove that they too are imperfect.

The Bible does not say that there should never be judging. There are instances in Scripture and, therefore, in our lives, when judging is appropriate and necessary. While the Bible strictly forbids us from judging each other for personal sins, God does allow the Church to judge sin that is impinging upon the moral or administrative life of the Church. Paul writes, *"It is reported commonly that there is fornication among you, and such fornication as is not so much as named among the Gentiles, that one should have his father's wife"* (1 Cor. 5:1). Here we have an incestuous relationship between a man and his stepmother. What does Paul recommend they do about it? Overlook it? No! He writes:

> *In the name of the Lord Jesus Christ, when ye are gathered together, and my spirit, with the power of our Lord Jesus Christ, to deliver such an one unto satan for the destruction of the flesh, that the spirit might be saved in the day of the Lord Jesus (1 Corinthians 5:4-5).*

To deliver this man over to satan means giving the enemy the right to smite and afflict him in whatever way he wants to. This is the same principle carried out in Job 2:6-7, when God turned Job over to satan. In the New Testament, judgmental authority resides in the Church. While we are examining this situation at Corinth, let us remember that the objective of the judgment was twofold: 1. to hinder sin in the church and 2. to keep the individual from losing his salvation. The fact that we do not judge each other for personal sins does not mean that people can live any way they want to among us and we have to tolerate it. The objective of judging is always to rectify. If we conclude that someone's sin has come before the church, we must judge. However, we never stop loving. We never stop helping. We never stop praying. We never stop hoping that that individual will get things right with God.

Whatever happened to the saint who was in that incestuous relationship? He was forgiven and restored to the church. Paul writes in Second Corinthians 2:6-8:

> *Sufficient to such a man is this punishment, which was inflicted of many. So contrariwise ye ought rather to forgive him, and comfort him, lest perhaps such a one should be swallowed up with overmuch sorrow. Wherefore, I beseech you that ye would confirm your love towards him.*

The Judgment Seat of Christ

Finally, whenever Paul dealt with the spirit of judging, he always defended the fact that the Lord shall ultimately judge us all. This is an important point and one that should put to rest the spirit of judgment among us. No matter what we do or what the motive might be for why we do it, ultimately we must all answer to the Lord for every act of sin. Whether it is murder or gossip, lying or gambling, sexual immorality or pride, we shall all stand before the judgment seat of Christ to answer to God for it. Paul writes in Romans 14:10, *"But why doest thou judge thy brother? Or why dost thou set at naught thy brother? For we must all stand before the judgment seat of Christ."* It is interesting to note here how Paul offers this judgment seat of Christ as a conclusion to the spirit of judgment. He seems to suggest that the reality that we will answer to the Lord should give us peace about one another's faults—not in the sense that we tolerate sin or refuse to preach against sin. It simply removes the need to judge or feel like we need to punish someone for their shortcomings. Praise God, the judgment seat of Christ has taken away my need to judge.

Endnotes

1. John C. Maxwell, *There's No Such Thing as "Business" Ethics: There's Only One Rule For Making Decisions* (New York, NY: Warner, 2003), 9.

2. *The Merriam-Webster Dictionary* (Springfield, MA: Merriam Webster Inc., 1997), s.v. "judge."

3. Derek Prince, *Judging: When? Why? How?* (New Kensington, PA: Whitaker House, 2001), 39-43.

4. *The Merriam-Webster Dictionary*, s.v. "contempt."

Chapter 8

Competitive Jealousy

By the blessing of the upright the city is exalted: but it is overthrown by the mouth of the wicked (Proverbs 11:11).

ONE OF THE greatest motivators of gossip is our own ambition. Therefore, in order to overcome gossip, we must get a grip on who we are and how we accomplish our goals. We must understand the inner motivations behind the things we do. A friend of mine is a middle school teacher. One day we were talking together, and he began to share with me that he often had to avoid a certain coworker. The reason he would avoid him was that this man always had something bad to say about the principal of the school. My friend went on to tell me that his coworker was a Christian man and that he did not understand why he was not convicted about the gossip he was spreading about this principal. Then, as if he had received a revelation from God, he said, "Well, I do know why he gossips about her—he wants her job." In this way, competitive jealousy becomes a great motivator for gossip. Many Christians don't even realize when they are enraptured with competitive jealousy. This chapter is written to help us get a grip on an enemy of the Christian life called competitive jealousy.

Before we can properly tackle the matter of competitive jealousy, we must first give a definition to the phrase. The word *competitive* has as its root the word *compete*. We all know what competition is. Many of us have competed and still today are competitors. To be competitive implies that there is someone or something in our lives that we seek to advance beyond. Competition can be good or bad depending upon the perspective and the context. While competition for an Olympic gold medal is good, competition between a husband and a wife can be bad. This is the essence of the word *competitive*.

The word *jealousy* means a sense of uneasiness or anxiety that stems from the fear of preference being given to another. It also refers to having stress or anxiety over the person or possessions of another. To be jealous means we are not satisfied and content with where we are, what we are doing, or what we possess. There is nothing inherently wrong with being dissatisfied with how much money or personal possessions we have. However, something is wrong when we become dissatisfied only when we see how much someone else has. There is nothing wrong with making an honest assessment of ourselves and seeing things about ourselves that we would like to change. There is something wrong when our self-assessment diminishes when we compare ourselves to others.

If we take the powerful drive of competitiveness and combine it with the volatile poison of jealousy, this synergy creates a lethal formula we call *competitive jealousy*. Competitive jealousy is an attitude or spirit that a person assumes. It is totally antithetical to the way of the Cross and totally insensitive to the Lordship of Jesus Christ.

The first instance of competitive jealousy happened many ages ago. We can read about it in the 14th chapter of the Book of Isaiah,

> *How art thou fallen from heaven, O Lucifer, son of the morning? How art thou cut down to the ground, which didst weaken the nations? For thou hast said in thine heart, "I will ascend into heaven, I will exalt my throne above the stars of God: I will sit also upon the Mount of the congregation, in the sides of the north: I will ascend above the heights of the clouds; I will be like the Most High." Yet thou shalt be brought down to hell, to the sides of the pit* (Isaiah 14:12-15).

What happened many years ago was that satan began to compare what he had (all of which was given to him by God) to what God had. The spirit of competitive jealousy then ensued, and although satan had much, he became discontent. His heart was changed, and in his misery, he began to seek to compete with God. We can see from the above text that satan was ruling over nations down here on earth, for the above Scripture says, *"which didst weaken the nations."* We can also see from the above text that he also had access to Heaven, for it reads, *"I will ascend into heaven."* Satan coveted the things he saw that God possessed when he went into the heavens to make his reports to God. He then concluded that he would take them from God. Satan declared, *"I will ascend into heaven, I will exalt my throne...I will be like the Most High."* Yet the prophet tells us what satan's competitive spirit brought him.

In God's own words, *"Thou shalt be brought down to hell, to the sides of the pit."* This is the first record of the spirit of competitive jealousy. The accuser spirit is also a spirit of jealousy. We are never acting more like satan than when we are caught up in the ravages of gossip because of the spirit of competitive jealousy.

We can see the spirit of competitive jealousy manifested throughout the Bible. In Genesis chapter 37, Joseph's brothers allowed the enemy to use the spirit of competitive jealousy to cause them to harm their own brother. We read in Genesis 37:3-4,

> *Now Israel loved Joseph more than all his children, because he was the son of his old age: and he made him a coat of many colors. And when his brethren saw that their father loved him more than all his brethren, they hated him, and could not speak peaceably unto him.*

As soon as Joseph's brothers saw that he had obtained favor or blessing that they did not possess, they become jealous. Then in the spirit of competitive jealousy, they set out to disadvantage him. We all know the story; they took him and cast him into a pit. Then they sold him to a company of Ishmealites going down to Egypt. All this they did out of competitive jealousy. If Christians do not watch their hearts concerning other people's successes, possessions, or blessings, the enemy will use this spirit to destroy the very fabric of their walk with Christ.

Competitive jealousy drives people to compare their clothes, their house, their car, their financial position, their attainment, even themselves to other people. As we have seen with satan, as well as with Joseph's brothers, once the comparison begins, the next step is competition for position, for power, for authority, or for influence. For instance, although God has blessed one person with a nice 2005 Ford, every time he sees his neighbor getting into a 2012 Mercedes, he gets jealous. What's more is that he now doesn't seem to like that neighbor as much since he got the Mercedes. This same person has another neighbor who drives a 1988 Honda, but he never seems to get the same jealous spirit concerning that neighbor.

Competitive jealousy keeps people from appreciating one another. In America there is a tremendous drive toward materialistic success. This pull can become a burden on the Christian walk. We may always be striving for that new car or new house and asking God to join us in our quest while ignoring what He wants to accomplish in our lives and hearts. Many Christians live far above their means, stretching their budgets and their credit cards to the limit as they strive to keep up with "Mr. and Mrs. Jones." Speaking of Mrs. Jones, some of us hold contempt for her in our hearts because she and her husband moved into the new subdivision. Their home cost three times as much as ours, and we think she flaunts the fact that she has a little something. We go out of our way on Sunday mornings not to sit next to her in church, and we often rehearse her faults with others. But the truth is, God is not dissatisfied with her; He is dissatisfied with us. We should be more mature in our Christian walk by now. We should have grown beyond these petty, materialistic strivings, but instead of pressing in toward God, we have allowed worldliness to ensnare us.

There is another American mandate that promotes competitive jealousy. It involves the television promotions of the perfect body. Glamorous models are presented on television as the ideal image and body. Hollywood's image of a woman is 20 years old, 97 pounds, with long hair, smooth skin, and glimmering teeth.

Images of the perfect woman (or man) only place heavy burdens upon us and cause us to lose our focus on Jesus Christ. This leads to unnecessary depression and low self-image in Christian women and men alike. We all admire the images—they are beautiful—but life is not about the images. Paul said, *"To live is Christ"* (Phil. 1:21). Life for him was first and foremost a matter of his relationship with Jesus, not his image before people.

I believe in being a good steward over my body. I also believe God is a God of prosperity. However, I am grounded by the words of Jesus when He said, *"For what is a man profited, if he shall gain the whole world, and lose his soul? Or what shall a man give in exchange for his soul?"* (Matt. 16:26). What will we profit if we gain the perfect body, the largest house, and the most expensive car, yet have a front row seat in hell? It is all about setting our priorities in life and knowing what is important. In an effort to keep up with the materialistic American ideal, many Christians have become shipwrecked, learning to embrace this world more than the one that is to come. They have lost the Lord in the competition for status and distinction in this world.

Worldliness

Love not the world, neither the things that are in the world. If any man love the world, the love of the Father is not in him (1 John 2:15).

Competitive jealousy is driven by worldliness. Most Christians today have never heard of such a word as *worldliness*. This is probably because many of today's preachers are worldly. Worldliness is having a propensity and predisposition for the things of this world. Worldliness causes Christians to place the pursuits of this world ahead of their relationship with God. This world and the things in it become "gods" to them. That means things like money, cars, houses, pleasure, fame, and recognition all resonate in their souls and have deposed Christ as Lord of their lives. The Bible says, *"The love of money is the root of all evil..."* (1 Tim. 6:10). You can be poor, even broke, and love money. There are poor people who love money, and there are rich people who don't.

The love of money is only one of the signs of a worldly person. Jesus our Lord calls us to deny ourselves, take up our cross, and follow Him (see Matt. 16:24). This is not a mandate to be poor, but it is a mandate not to be worldly. Television has perverted the perspective of many people, leading them to believe that to be a Christian is only a matter of whether you go to church or not. The call of the Christian life is *sanctification*. This word means to be set apart. We are called to be holy, even as our Father in Heaven is holy. Today, unfortunately, we cannot distinguish most Christians from the world, especially in conversation. Their gossiping tongues and competitive spirits belie the fact that they are believers.

Covetousness

*For this ye know, that no whoremonger, nor unclean person, **nor covetous man, who is an idolater,** hath any inheritance in the kingdom of Christ and of God* (Ephesians 5:5).

*Mortify therefore your members which are upon the earth; fornication, uncleanness, inordinate affection, evil concupiscence, and **covetousness, which is idolatry.** For which things sake the wrath of God cometh on the children of disobedience* (Colossians 3:5-6).

And [Jesus] *said unto them, "Take heed, and **beware of covetousness**: for a man's life consisteth not in the abundance of the things which he possesseth"* (Luke 12:15).

To covet is to have a strong desire for something. When the Bible identifies people as covetous, it is because there is something here in this world that they pursue harder than they seek after Jesus Christ. The Word of God seems to make a definite connection between covetousness and idolatry. Most saints think of *idolatry* as an Old Testament word that refers to the Israelites carving out wooden statues for their houses. But all three of the above Scriptures deal with idolatry, and all three are New Testament Scriptures. Many Christians' hearts are idolatrous because they are full of excessive desire for things of this world. I once knew a man who had a problem overcoming sexual lust. He prayed and prayed for victory in this area. One day, while on vacation, God gave him the revelation that he was in idolatry. *What? In idolatry?* he thought to himself. That was the last thing he saw himself as. Thoughts ran through his head of people in the Old Testament who had house gods and of people who worshiped the moon and stars. That was idolatry in his mind. But the Lord began to show him that a covetous spirit drove his desire for women. The women he desired were idols to him. The Lord went on to show him that the entire pornography industry works by idolatry. If he wanted victory in the area of sexual lust, he had to first renounce the idol of the female body. This man did renounce it and got his victory.

God is displeased because there are many Christians today who are living in idolatry. For instance, living in a big house is much more important to many saints than doing God's will. Driving a nice car is much more important to them than supporting the Gospel by paying their tithes. They are idolaters; they worship the things of this world. There are many idolaters in the Church, men and women who would rather stay in the back and count money than hear the sermon on Sunday morning. They cannot come out to hear the Word of God being preached because they have to go back and worship their god. All covetousness is idolatry.

Since the three Scriptures I quoted above are New Testament Scriptures, I will close this section with an Old Testament scripture. Exodus 20:2-3 says, *"I am the Lord thy God, which have brought thee out of the land of Egypt, out of the house of bandage. Thou shalt have no other gods* [but] *Me."* When our quest for the things of this world has silenced the Holy Spirit in our lives, we have placed other gods before Him.

Competitive Jealousy in the Church

For we dare not make ourselves of the number, or compare ourselves with some that commend themselves: but they measuring themselves by themselves, and comparing themselves among themselves, are not wise (2 Corinthians 10:12).

Thus far I have been discussing competitive jealousy as a phenomenon in the individual's life. But what about the Church? Do we experience competitive jealousy in the Church? Of course we do. People in the corporate world spend much time and energy competing for ascendancy. They know that success has to be fought for and that all their dreams hinge upon making the next step up the ladder of success. Many in the Church are also trying to climb the "corporate spiritual ladder of success." This makes for much competition in the Church.

Some people's motivations for serving in the Church are as vain as those who serve in the world. Their personal agenda is to advance among and receive glory from people. Many have lost the sensitivity of hope in a future reward from God. Their spiritual eyes being dim, they strive for success in the church as if God has never promised to reward those who serve faithfully with good motives (see Rev. 22:12). Some rub elbows with the pastor, hoping to gain some special place in his heart and hopefully some special position in the church. Women may envy the pastor's wife, gossiping about her inadequacies. Lead singers in the choir are often in a tantrum because someone decided not to allow them to sing their favorite song. They storm out and leave the church when someone else is chosen to sing the opening song. The young assistant pastor cannot overcome the idea that he preaches a little better than the senior pastor. Church administrators become possessive of their job duties, seeking to vanquish everyone who desires a position of significance. The officers of the church can't get their eyes off the pulpit. They have control in every area of the church, but are still tormented by the fact that they are not the pastor. Is competitive jealousy in the Church? I would answer an emphatic "Yes!"

> *For ye are yet carnal: for whereas there is among you envying, and strife, and divisions, are ye not carnal, and walk as men?* (1 Corinthians 3:3)

In the Scripture above, Paul is dealing with competitive jealousy in the Corinthian church. The Corinthians were in a constant skirmish over who had the most authority and who was the most important. Paul writes to them and tells them they are carnal. This word *carnal* means to be led by the dictates of the flesh and not by the Holy Spirit. To be carnal means being ruled by lust, emotions, attitudes, or selfish interests and not by the Spirit of God. It is a spiritual slap in the face for Christians to be told they are carnal. But believe it or not, many in today's Church are carnal. Paul gives the proof of the Corinthian's carnality by pointing out the fact there was present *"envy, strife, and divisions."* I know of many churches today where these three things are highly present, yet no one has ever stopped to address the carnality. They don't even recognize that they are carnal.

Denominationalism

Now this I say, that every one of you saith, I am of Paul; and I of Apollos; and I of Cephas; and I of Christ. Is Christ divided? Was Paul crucified for you? Or were ye baptized in the name of Paul? (1 Corinthians 1:12-13).

For while one saith, I am of Paul; and another, I am of Apollos; are ye not carnal? Who then is Paul, and who is Apollos, but ministers by whom ye believed, even as the Lord gave to every man? I have planted, Apollos watered; but God gave the increase. So then neither is he that planteth anything, neither he that watereth; but God that giveth the increase (1 Corinthians 3:4-7).

The Corinthian church had a big problem with division and jealousy. Twice in the first letter to the Corinthians, Paul notes that they were divided over who had birthed them into Christ. It is carnality that gets people into examining what makes one person better than the other. These Corinthians were debating with each other saying, *"I am of Paul,"* that is to say, "Paul is my spiritual father." Others were saying, *"I am of Apollos," "I am of Cephas* [Peter]," *"I am of Christ."* Now of course, there were people there at Corinth who had been born again by the witness of their local pastor and even by the witness of laymen who shared their faith with others. The claiming of Paul, Apollos, and Cephas was a sort of badge of honor—a way of signifying that they were better than those who had been born again by the mere witness of the local elders and pastors.

We might be inclined to think that the competitive jealousy of the Corinthian church was ridiculous until we come to realize that we today are the same way. Instead of using Paul, Apollos, and Peter, let us insert our denominational preferences and see if the Church today is not carnal.

> *Now this I say, that every one of you saith, I am* [Baptist]; *and I* [Methodist]; *and I* [Holiness]; *and I* [Charismatic-Full Gospel]. *Is Christ divided?* (based on 1 Corinthians 1:12-13)

Is the Church today really different from the early Church? Are we really free from competitive jealousy? I think not. Most of the saints today cannot stomach the thought that God does not hold their particular denomination in special regard. It is time for the saints to mature and to realize that the Lord did not start any denominations. On the contrary, His priestly prayer was that His Church would be one (see John 17:9-11).

Many of the saints show special preference in regard to gossip and evil reporting. If individuals are not from their denomination, they don't mind gossiping, slandering, and evil reporting about them. However, those individuals who are of their own sect, they protect. This shows our carnality and immaturity, and it also shows that we are not in submission to the Lord. It is carnal to be bent on the development of a certain group or section of the Body of Christ at the expense of the rest of the Church. One of the signs that we have not come into full maturity is the reality that churches today see one another as "the competition." For this reason, we cannot rejoice with one another about spiritual victories or celebrate one another's ministries. Unfortunately, this attitude is buttressed by pastors who insist on viewing ministry as if they were the only ones whom God has called to preach. It is time we realized that spiritual victory at any church is victory for the entire Body of Christ. If someone's church takes in a member or someone gets born again at any church, we can all celebrate because satan has lost one more soul. May we all gain enough maturity to celebrate one another's ministries.

The Spirit of Discredit

Competitive jealousy fuels another sinister evil called the spirit of discredit. The gist of this spirit is that when Christian people become competitive with each other, they often become resistant to the success of one another. We all desire to be successful; it is an inherent drive within us all. And we usually transfer that desire for success to our churches. Unaware that the accuser is very aware of our ambitions for ourselves and for our churches, we can easily become tools for the enemy. Ambitious Christians who are jealous of other believers' gifts and callings will often take on a discrediting campaign against other Christians.

Here is an example. One day two Christian women are sitting in McDonalds talking, and one woman says to the other, "Pastor

Walker from Overcoming Life Church preached at our church last Sunday, and God really used him. His message was so powerful, and it blessed all of us." The woman she is speaking to attends another church in town. Instead of simply acknowledging and praising God with her friend, the other woman, moved with envy, responds, "He ain't right. I heard he has a lot of skeletons in his closet." By saying this, the second woman endeavors to discredit the man's ministry instead of acknowledging that God has used him. Here is another example: A certain woman has an awesome ability to sing. She offers her gift to the local church and is quickly promoted to the head of the music ministry. The saints in the congregation, however, are reluctant to receive her gift. Instead of receiving and acknowledging her gift, the other choir members say, "She has been married three or four times." By doing this, they discredit her ministry and work against the plan of God.

The spirit of discredit is used so often in the Church. I know of a man who preached powerfully on the subject of prosperity. The spirit of God was using him to help the saints get their financial breakthrough. But throughout the town, Christians were saying, "He is just greedy for money." This is the accuser's work of discrediting ministry. The enemy knows that if people respect and accept the gifts God sends, his program will be broken and people will be set free. But because there are so many ambitious and competitive saints, he can easily employ Christians to gossip against one another and to discredit one another's ministries. We will all have to come to the reality that God uses imperfect people. We will also have to acknowledge that our promotion in ministry will come from God and not from our selfish ambitions. The Word of God says, *"Humble yourselves therefore under the mighty hand of God, that He may exalt you in due time"* (1 Pet. 5:6).

Gaining Victory Over Competitive Jealousy

The only book I have ever read on this subject of competitive jealousy was by Creflo A. Dollar Jr. The title of the book is *Exposing The Spirit of Competitive Jealousy*.[1] In the book, Pastor Dollar offers eight steps to overcoming this spirit. I will list each of the eight steps below and expound on them with explanation and examples of my own for your clarification and edification.

Step One: Take Stock of Your Motives

Every Christian should learn the Scripture that says, *"Man looks at the outward appearance, but the Lord looks at the heart"* (1 Sam. 16:7 NKJV). Once we begin to recognize God's omniscience, it helps us realize that we don't have to do any outward act in order to sin. Upon gaining this understanding, we begin to scrutinize more closely our inner state. Jesus taught us that sin is to be dealt with from within. Christians do not—or should not—have to police outward acts of sin, because we are constantly addressing sin at its roots within our hearts. The first step in gaining the victory over competitive jealousy is to begin to ask ourselves, "Why do I do the things I do?" or "Why do I feel the way I do?" If our motives are competition or jealousy, then we must repent.

Let me give a very simple example. A minister may be sitting near the pulpit while another preacher is preaching. He begins to feel uneasy, and he begins to have a judgmental attitude toward the man who is ministering. As he questions his own motives, he realizes that in his heart he does not want this man to preach well. Why? Because he believes the other man is a better preacher, and he does not want his members to hear another preacher out preach him. Instead of allowing sin to rule in his heart, he quietly repents and asks God to bless the man's message. By doing this, he crucifies sin at the root. Checking our motives is a continual process in the Christian life that keeps us humble before the Lord and godly before the world.

Step Two: Learn to Repent

When we find areas of our lives where we have been influenced by competitive jealousy, we should immediately repent. Here is a good example: A young woman's attitude has been totally wrong since her girlfriend got engaged. Her friend found the type of guy the young woman always dreamed of. Since the engagement, the young woman has not called or stopped by her friend's house. She told her it was because she has been busy, but her true motive was to punish her by causing her to lose a friendship at the expense of a relationship. Her motive is wrong. She should repent for separating from her friend and renew their friendship. Repentance is a continual part of the Christian walk. Without repentance, we would lose our fellowship with God. When we have been contaminated by the spirit of competitive jealousy, repentance is the step we need to take to return to fellowship with God.

Step Three: Exercise Authority Over Jealousy in Your Life

The Word of God tells us that we have authority in Jesus' name over every evil spirit (see Matt. 10:1). We have authority in His name not to be under the control of the spirit of jealousy. When our moods and attitudes are being controlled by circumstances around us, the Holy Spirit is not ruling in us. For this reason, we must take authority over our lives in the name of Jesus. Nothing should control us but God.

Step Four: Gain God's Perspective

As we get more understanding of this malicious spirit of competitive jealousy from the Word of God, we can begin to pray and ask God to give us His perspective on life. How would God have us view the person who got the promotion? How would God have us view the church down the street? How would God have us view other men and women of God? When we begin to see things from God's vantage point, we will no longer desire to see it from the world's view. We will also begin to see ourselves from God's perspective. This means understanding that what we have and what we don't have has all been divinely appointed. It's not that we cannot increase in possessions, but we must understand that God wants us to prosper even as our souls prosper (see 3 John 2). As we are renewing our minds on this very issue of competitive jealousy, we are positioning ourselves for promotion.

Step Five: Guard Your Heart

Guarding our hearts means setting a watch on what we see and what we hear. We must learn to watch our perspectives. When we sense that we have started to compare ourselves to others, we must abandon the thought altogether. There should be no place in our lives for competitive comparison. We should learn to *"be content with such things as ye have"* (Heb. 13:5). We must stop comparing our hairstyles, our cars, our houses, our bodies, or anything else we have with other people. We must be content with what God has given us. We must wear what we wear, drive what we drive, minister like we minister, do what we do, look like we look, and let the peace of God rule in our hearts and minds.

Step Six: Major on Being a Servant

Jesus said in Matthew 23:12, *"And whosoever shall exalt himself shall be abased; and he that shall humble himself shall be exalted."* Understanding this should cause us to realize that the way up is down. The spirit of competitive jealousy causes people to want to exalt themselves above others. Therefore, to overcome this spirit, we should make it our life objective to be a servant. First Peter 5:6 says, *"Humble yourselves therefore under the mighty hand of God, that He may exalt you in due time."* If we humble ourselves and wait on God, He will see to it that we shine. It is better to shine because God is showing us off, than to shine because of our own personal ambitions. God has not forgotten us. If we will be patient, He will raise us up in due time.

Step Seven: Be Glad When Others Are Blessed

Instead of speaking evil of people because they get a blessing, let us learn to rejoice with them. The Word of God says, *"Rejoice with those who rejoice..."* (Rom. 12:15 NKJV). We are often guilty of holding contempt for those who rejoice. When our friends or neighbors get a blessing, we must not become discouraged, but rather "shout and stay in line." Our day is coming. But if we fail to shout with our sisters and brothers, it means jealousy has caused us to get out of line.

We should not get caught up in asking, "Why is God blessing them and not me?" or in analysis of who "deserves" the blessing and who "does not deserve" the blessing, based on human standards of righteousness. If we are thinking like that, we will always be outside the loop of God's blessings. God does not bless on a scale of who's good and who's bad. God will release grace into our lives based on holy living, but He does not bless His children based on human standards of righteousness. What sort of parents would let one of their children eat dinner while making the other go hungry because one was more obedient than the other? When Christmas comes around, all of the children get gifts, no matter how good or bad they have been. My point here is that we don't bless our children on a sliding scale because they are our children. Therefore, we should be glad when God blesses one of His children, and we will find that we will make it to the front of the line a lot faster.

Step Eight: Build Confidence in God's Love for You

Often when we are waiting on God for a blessing, the enemy will try to make us feel that God does not love us. This is to weaken our faith and allow discouragements to come in. We must build our faith in God through the study of His Word. For there in His Word He commends His love toward us through the teachings of Jesus Christ (see John 3:16-17). Praise and worship is another way of building up our "love bank" with God. As we express our love for God through praise and worship, God commends His love toward us in the Spirit. He confirms within our spirits that He loves us and has the best in mind for us.

Endnote

1. Creflo Dollar Jr., *Exposing the Spirit of Competitive Jealousy* (Edmond, OK: Vision Communication, 1993), 24-27.

Chapter 9

Forgiveness

Whatever good you do is remembered by God and forgotten by people; whatever bad you do is forgotten by God and remembered by people.

THERE WAS A certain woman who never had anything good to say about her mother. She was always putting her down and gossiping about her poor parenting skills. Suddenly, this daughter started having problems with her health. Her doctor could not find anything physiologically wrong with her, so he recommended she see a psychiatrist. She spent the next two years with a psychiatrist, trying to figure out why her health was failing. After two years of counseling and $40,000 worth of medical bills and prescription medications, the psychiatrist spoke these words to her: "I have learned enough about you to deduce that your condition stems from your relationship with your mother. Yet, I don't feel you are working with me. In order for us to get you healed and feeling better, you are going to have to forgive your mother—and your stepfather." As it turned out, her illness was precipitated by her failure to forgive her mother and stepfather for things that had long since passed. A Bible-believing pastor who taught biblical forgiveness could have saved her $40,000 and a lot of stress.

Unforgiveness is one of the greatest "cancers" the world has ever known. But there is good news—it is curable.

> *For if ye forgive men their trespasses, your heavenly Father will also forgive you. But if ye forgive not men their trespasses, neither will your Father forgive your trespasses* (Matthew 6:14-15).

I honestly believe that anytime gossip and evil speaking become rampant in a church, home, business, or community, it is a sign that people aren't forgiving. Unforgiveness becomes the fuel that keeps the fires of negative speech burning. Because true forgiveness is so rare these days, it is no wonder Christians often find staying away from gossip to be quite difficult. Every time we open our mouths to address the personal lives of other people, we should ask ourselves the question, "Have I forgiven the person I am speaking about?" If we have truly forgiven them, there is no need to speak ill of them.

Tragically enough, many Christian people tend to view forgiveness as something honorable, but optional. Many saints have a Hollywood perspective of forgiveness. It is the kind of disposition that says we can forgive our enemies every once in a while, but most of the time, we kill them. This is a false view of forgiveness. A proper biblical view of forgiveness is that it is both obligatory and indispensable. We must move forgiveness from being a moral option to being what it actually is—a biblical doctrine. All doctrine in Scripture is of supreme importance and weight. For instance, the shed blood of Jesus for the remissions of sins is not just a biblical teaching, but also a biblical doctrine. Because it is a doctrine, it is indispensable to the faith and mandatory to the teaching of Christian living. Forgiveness is also a biblical doctrine, essential to living the Christian life.

One of the hallmarks of being a Christian should be the fact that we, unlike people of other religions, and unlike the unsaved, are practitioners of forgiveness. God even saved us by forgiving our sins. In the above passage, Jesus gives great weight to forgiveness, placing it as a stipulation to the remission of our own sins. He says, *"If ye forgive not..., **neither** will your Father forgive your trespasses"* (Matt. 6:15). If gossip is an indicator of unforgiveness, and unforgiveness is an indication that people's sins have not been forgiven, this means that there are some entire churches, cities, and nations that are yet in their sins. We acknowledge that often gossip happens because someone has sinned, but we also confirm that it continues because someone refuses to forgive.

In the federal prison system, if a convicted criminal comes in with a life sentence, he is going to spend a minimum of 25 years in prison before he is eligible for parole. However, if he has good behavior, goes to church, and is diligent in his work, the guards may make a report of his good behavior, and the warden of the prison may have the life sentence modified. This happened while a friend of mine was in prison. He told me that he knew a man who had killed both his wife and another man. He had to serve two 25 year sentences. He was ordered to serve 25 years minimum before he was eligible for parole. When the man came into the prison, however, he became a converted Christian. The guards, noticing his willing attitude and hard-working disposition, went to the warden and told the warden of the prison about the man's change. The parole board had the life sentences lifted, and the man was home in 15 years. Now if the prison system will show mercy and forgiveness toward a man who is a convicted murderer, the Church cannot lag behind in its disposition to forgive.

R.T. Kendall, in his book *Total Forgiveness,* mentions the fact that Nelson Mandela is perhaps the best example in the 20th century of a man who has taught us how to forgive. After 27 years of political incarceration—the longest serving political prisoner in the world at that time—he emerged unscathed and told his people to forgive their oppressors, to focus on the future, and to work toward building a new, united nation. In spite of the devastating trauma of apartheid, Mandela chose the path of forgiveness and reconciliation rather than the policy of revenge and vindictiveness. For people who are seeking to come to terms with a history of oppression, conflict, and disagreement, for people who have reached the rock bottom of despair and despondency, this was the best advice he could have given because "there can be no future without forgiveness."[1]

Third Party Forgiveness

Bear with each other and forgive whatever grievances you may have against one another. Forgive as the Lord forgave you (Colossians 3:13 NIV).

When it comes to forgiveness, there is a first, second, and third party reality. The first party is the person who brings the sin, crime, or offense. The second party is the person who has been offended or hurt. However, sometimes both of these parties have been offended with each other. We may have an instance where *party one* lies to *party two,* and the lie is hurtful for the second individual. Here we employ Christ's teaching, telling the individuals involved that they must forgive. Jesus said, *"For if ye forgive men their trespasses, your heavenly Father will also forgive you your trespasses"* (Matt. 6:14). The lie may have been hurtful. Maybe it damaged a person's reputation. Regardless of the pain, we are to forgive.

We almost always seem to think of forgiveness in the first party or second party terms. However, there is a third party forgiveness that we all experience from time to time. Third party forgiveness is just as important as first and second party forgiveness. Often people fail to forgive in third party situations. Since the crime or action was not directed at them, they feel that it is not necessary for them to forgive. An example of this would be if a woman is raped. The rapist is the first party bringing offense and needing forgiveness. The woman is the second party needing to forgive (this does not always mean that legal charges are dropped; God ordained the law). The third party is the woman's family. One of the problems in third party forgiveness is that the third party tends to see themselves as the judge, instead of realizing that even though they were not acted on directly, they still must forgive.

The Scripture above says, *"Forgive whatever grievances you may have against one another. Forgive as the Lord forgave you"* (Col. 3:13 NIV). When this woman's family thinks about how she was hurt and violated, they become angry. They have hostility and hate in their hearts toward the rapist because of what he did. Because they see themselves as judges bringing a verdict against him, they may be blind to their need to forgive him. The Scripture says, *"Forgive whatever grievances...."* This means that whatever has been done, even if it was not directly related to us, we must forgive. This is third party forgiveness. Jesus has not only forgiven us of our offenses against Him, but He has also forgiven us of our offenses toward one another. This is what Isaiah was referring to when he wrote, *"the chastisement of our peace was upon him"* (Isa. 53:5). For us to have peace with God and with one another, Jesus was wounded. Third party forgiveness is extremely important.

I know of a church where the pastor offended a certain church member, and as a result, the church as a whole (the third party) held it against him for years. Someone asked me concerning this situation, "Why won't they just forgive their pastor? They know the Scriptures teach forgiveness." As I have said before, third parties often get caught up in judging and fail to forgive. This is why the Scriptures say that if we will not forgive people their trespasses, neither will our heavenly Father forgive us our trespasses (see Matt. 6:15). This principle applies to all forgiveness—first, second, and third party.

Defining Forgiveness

When we speak of forgiveness, let us be clear what forgiveness is not. The following are some of the aspects of forgiveness that should be understood by those who would practice forgiveness.

1. Forgiveness does not mean approving of what the person did.

Forgiving someone does not mean approving of what was done. God never approved of Adam and Eve's sin in the Garden of Eden. On the contrary, He drove them out of the garden. However, He shows us the symbol of His forgiveness in making animal skins for them to cover their nakedness (see Gen. 3:21). In the New Testament, Jesus forgave the woman caught in adultery, but He did not approve of the sin, telling her, *"...Go and sin no more"* (John 8:11). When we approve of sin, we validate the culprit's misdeeds and lead that individual to feel like it is OK to do the same thing again. We must learn to emphatically denounce the wrong that has been done, while yet forgiving as if the deed had not been done.

2. Forgiveness does not mean closing our eyes to those who would continually bring harm to us or others.

One of the most basic tenets of forgiveness is that, before we can properly forgive, we must first remove ourselves from harm's way. Sometimes forgiveness must be "one-sided." This means that the other party involved has either not forgiven, will not forgive, or does not have an understanding of forgiveness. If this is the case, the other parties in the offense with us may still be hostile toward us. The first step to forgiveness then would be to separate from them in order to keep ourselves from continued harm. Then, in the safety of moving to another place or position, we can properly forgive. If we see children or people we know in a position where someone is taking advantage of them, we should not rest until we have removed them from the potential danger. After the danger is removed or they have been removed from that person's access, we should then become advocates of forgiveness.

3. Forgiveness is not excusing, justifying, or denying what has been done.

It is not our job to cover up the sins of other people. We have absolutely no obligation to attempt to explain why a wrong was done. To endorse a sinful act is blasphemy. Neither do we "justify" the sin by trying to somehow make it "OK." God does not call sin "right," and neither should we. Also, it is important that we not deny what has been done. In order to forgive, some people decide to act as if the offense did not take place. This sort of repression does not help at all. Although it may be painful to face the facts, healing and truth are inseparable. True forgiveness is realizing the seriousness of the infraction, but deciding to be like your heavenly Father who, though our sins were serious, chose to forgive us.

4. *Forgiveness is not always pardoning the offense.*

We should note that, although we are responsible for forgiving our brothers and sisters, we are not responsible for any offense against the law. For the law is a judge in and of itself. If we run a traffic light, we should not appeal to the officer for forgiveness, because the offense is not against the officer, but against the law. Even God was not able to pardon us when we as sinners offended the law, but instead He sent a substitute to accept the punishment for us in Jesus Christ. For this reason, any offense against the law must be faced.

If a person kills a couple's son, they will need to forgive. However, that person has offended the law. The parents had nothing to do with the establishment of the law; therefore, they have nothing to do with the offender's need to face the law. We must understand that the law does not forgive, but we must. If someone steals, they have broken the law, and they must face the law. The law does not forgive, but the person who was stolen from will ultimately have to practice forgiveness. The person who was stolen from may have to testify in court against the thief, yet still must practice forgiveness, because forgiveness is not approving of what a person does wrong.

Many Christians make the error of believing that they have some responsibility to both forgive and deliver offenders from their offense against the law. This is totally not the case. However, if an offense has occurred and the law gives us the responsibility of deciding whether to punish or absolve the offender, the decision is totally up to us. I have seen people forgive someone of even the legal responsibility for their sin. I believe that there are times when this is quite a noble act. I also believe there are times when the person needs to face punishment. We must remember, however, that punishment is not an excuse for failing to forgive.

5. *Forgiveness does not mandate reconciliation.*

Reconciliation implies the restoration of friendship or relationship after a quarrel. When a disgruntled husband and wife truly forgive, it will usually result in reconciliation. This is not, however, the case in every situation. Reconciliation requires the participation of two people. Often forgiveness has only occurred on one side of the issue. If two friends have fallen into conflict, one may reach a point of forgiveness before the other friend does. In some cases, one person in the conflict may have passed away since the time of the offense. This does not mean the other person cannot forgive. Jesus died for the sins of the whole world, although we were not physically present when He died. However, not everyone chooses to be reconciled to the people they have had offense with.

If we have truly forgiven those who have offended us, this may need to suffice in many situations. If a man's best friend sleeps with his wife, he will have to forgive, but he may not want his former best friend to come over for dinner on Wednesday nights. If a woman had access to a girlfriend's apartment and robs her blind, the girlfriend may not want her to keep the extra set of keys to her apartment any longer. It would be foolish for her to say, "I am going to forgive her, and to prove it, I won't even change my door locks." She might regret that! In situations like these, the restoration of the former relationship is sometimes impossible. Reconciliation is potential, but not mandatory.

6. Forgiveness does not mean forgetting.

I want to share a little secret. The Bible does not require us to "forgive and forget." This is a phrase people have created to try to signify the character of forgiveness. This phrase, however, has put many people in bondage, making them feel like they really have not forgiven unless and until they forget the incident. We are not humanly designed to forget significant events in our lives. If our minds were like chalkboards and could easily be erased, forgetting would be understandable, but the truth is that our minds do not work that way. The next time people say, "forgive and forget," we should tell them to take a hammer, crack open their skull, rub an eraser against their brain, and see if it works.

Forgiveness is not necessarily forgetting. Forgiveness is treating the people who offended us as if the offense never happened, despite the fact that we remember it. Of course, remembering sometimes comes with all of the attendant emotions of pain, resentment, and anger associated with the infraction. Forgiveness means that we choose to deny these negative feelings associated with what happened to us, believing that God will replace them with love for the individuals. Forgiveness is resolving that, even if it takes us a long time to change emotionally about the situation, we won't dwell on it. We will always treat the people we have forgiven in every respect like the offence has never occurred. Forgiveness is not forgetting; it is choosing not to remember.

What Forgiveness Is

Thus far, we have looked at some things forgiveness is not. Now I want to look at a few areas of what forgiveness *is*. The areas I deal with here are areas many people seem to have difficulty with.

1. Forgiveness is not gossiping about or slandering the individuals who offended us.

When people go through difficult or traumatic experiences, there is often a need to talk about it or share it with someone. This catharsis can be therapeutic. However, talking about what others have done to us can also be an avenue of revenge. The accuser takes advantage of offenses to create more offense. When people offend us, the accuser wants to use our story to cause others to be offended with the people who offended us. This is why it is important to note that people who truly forgive do not gossip about their offenders. Talking about how we have been offended with the purpose of hurting our enemy's reputation or credibility is just another form of revenge and is evidence that we have not forgiven.

God has said in His Word, *"'Vengeance is Mine, I will repay,' saith the Lord"* (Rom. 12:19). This applies even to attempts to defame people by gossiping about them. Forgiveness means that people are released from all punishment, not just some forms of punishment. A girlfriend did us wrong. We were hurt by it, but we decided we would forgive her. We said we were not going to beat her up, and we said we were not going to shoot her, so now we must stop trying to punish her with our tongues, and instead, pray for her success in life.

2. *Forgiveness means forgiving God.*

This may sound a little strange, but many people need to forgive God. For many people, life has not always gone their way. They have had some difficult circumstances and some unexplainable experiences. What happens to the young boy who, while trying to help a neighbor's child get out of the street, is struck by a car and permanently maimed? Day in and day out, he thinks to himself, *Why did God allow this to happen to me?* For many people, their story is not nearly as lamentable as this one, yet their sentiments are the same. The Christian wife with three kids whose husband runs off with another woman may sit in bitter contempt for her husband and for God. She had given her all to her marriage, and now she wants to know why God would allow her husband to do that to her.

I can give you many similar stories, but the bottom line is that we often blame God for the negative circumstances that happen in our lives. The enemy then comes in and attaches himself to our bitterness, pulling us away from the Lord who loves us. I have known people who blamed God for the death of their children, for their inability to get a job, even for their drug addiction. After all, they think, He is the one who allows bad things to happen to good people. He is all-powerful and all-knowing, and He could have prevented this tragedy. This type of rationale lands us in a quagmire of unforgiveness toward God.

I will not here attempt to defend God from His bitter enemies. Neither will I attempt to explain why God allows bad things to happen to good people (I really don't even believe He allows or disallows them). The only defense I offer is that the suffering of His Son Jesus is the greatest example of hardship the world has ever known. Jesus' suffering dwarfs other issues in comparison.

He took upon Himself the sins of the whole world. Even the sins of those who are bitter and resentful toward Him were punished in Himself.

He suffered more than we ever will, and He did it so that when we get to Heaven, we can get our family member back. We can get our house back. We can get our legs and feet back. He did it so that even if we don't get healed in this life, we will receive resurrection bodies in the life to come. He did it so that we can make it despite the husband who abandoned us. He died that we might have life (see John 10:10). He became sin so that we might be made the righteousness of God in Him (see 2 Cor. 5:21). He suffered so that we would have a blessed hope in His name. Glory to the name of Jesus. For this cause, my brothers and sisters, we must forgive God. He's not in Heaven bitter at us, so why should we be on earth bitter at Him? If there is such a thing as forgiving God, we should certainly do it.

3. *Forgiveness means forgiving ourselves.*

Some people's greatest battle has been about forgiving their enemies. Others have had to deal with bitterness and unforgiveness toward God. But there is another group of individuals whose greatest battle has been that of forgiving themselves. There is no lasting joy in forgiveness if it does not include ourselves. Some of us with the hardest time forgiving ourselves are those who have set high standards in our lives and have fallen short of them. Maybe we said we would never divorce, but today we are two-time divorcees. Maybe we set lofty standards for our lives, and we have accomplished none of them because of stupid choices. Maybe someone victimized us, and we feel like there were things we did that we should not have done. Maybe we listened to wicked people who got us into a lot of trouble. How we got where we are is not important. The thing that is important is what we do with the situation we are in.

The starting point, however, is not our situation, but ourselves. The first reality is that if we ask God to forgive us, He forgives us immediately and totally. The second reality is that we must not hold the matter against ourselves. Yes, we blew it, but life is not over. We must get up and start over. God has a plan for our lives. Why don't we give up the plans we had for our lives and ask God to give us His blueprints for the rest of our lives. We can't get caught up in how old we are or how many mistakes we have made.

I remember a church member of mine who was depressed. I asked her the reason for her depression. She said, "Well, pastor, I feel as if I could have done so much more for the Lord if I had accepted Him earlier in my life, but I was so rebellious!" I told her that Jesus is our example, and He finished God's work here on earth in three years. I asked her if she thought she would live another three years. She replied, "Of course I will live three years more if the Lord does not return." I said, "Well, let's get busy doing the will of God." We don't have time to waste; let's forgive ourselves and get on with our lives.

Why Forgive?

There was a certain man in the town that I live in whom I did not have a good attitude about. I had heard many things about him, most of which were negative. For years I avoided him and held contempt for him in my heart until God started dealing with me in this area of gossip and evil reporting. God began to show me that my attitude toward His child was wrong. He began to show me that I had no right to write anyone off on the basis of their faults because He had not written me off on the basis of my faults. I had to repent and ask God to forgive me for my disdain and negative attitude toward my Christian brother. I also asked God to forgive me for any gossip I had participated in with regard to this man.

When I did, God began to show me how satan was using unforgiveness and judging to keep the Body of Christ fragmented and weak. I realized then that I had to identify all of the people in my life whom I had separated from, ostracized, viewed with contempt, or gossiped about, and forgive them for the things they had done, even if they had not done those things against me. I realized that until and unless I forgave, I would not be forgiven. I also came to realize that oftentimes I thought it was people who were hindering me in life, when in actuality, it was my own negative prejudices toward others. God wants to give us new paradigms. He wants us to be able to see people the way He sees them. This can only happen when we humble ourselves and forgive whatever grievances we may have against others.

Brothers and sisters, let us forgive, for in forgiveness we birth greater possibilities for the amelioration and eradication of sin. Let us hope for a better day. Let us believe that by God's grace people can change. If I had no hope that I would be better tomorrow than I am today, I would despair. However, when I look at my life, I can see that I am more sanctified today than I was yesterday. Therefore, I have the hope that God will finish the work He has started in me. I believe that God is committed to changing others too. Despite all their mistakes, weaknesses, and foibles, God is committed to transforming them into the image of His Son Jesus. They are getting better, not worse.

The spirit of gossip and evil reporting assumes that individuals are and always will be the way they were in the past. It assumes people are hopelessly bound to particular sins. Even the Church has bought into the spirit of gossip, and therefore has ceased to strive to reform people and has instead resigned to talk about them. How unfortunate it is when those who have the life-changing Gospel and power of Jesus Christ—not to mention the Holy Spirit—sit and talk about the people they are sent to transform. The Bible describes the transformation of demoniacs, prostitutes, extortionists, divorcees, sorcerers, and murderers by the power of the Gospel. But because of lack of faith, we have offered God an evil report that says that people won't change and that even God can't change them. We have gone over to our Canaan and spied out the land, but instead of conquering it, we have decided to gossip about what we saw. Let us go back to faith and reclaim our status as the Church of the living God. Whether they are saved or unsaved, there is hope for the drunkard, the liar, the thief, the adulterer, the murderer, the homosexual, the slanderer, the gossip, the whisperer, and all others. Glory to the Lamb of God!

I believe there are three great hindrances to revival in America:

1. The saints must repent of gossiping against one another.

2. The saints must walk in love toward one another and show this love always in their daily conversations.

3. The saints must practice forgiveness, not only for faults and sins, but also for improper attitude.

Brothers and sisters, let us forgive. Through forgiveness we can heal a multitude of the things we talk about daily. Let us start at home by forgiving our family members. No longer can we speak negatively about our family. Husbands must forgive their wives, and wives must forgive their husbands. Pointing the finger of blame and speaking evil will never heal the family, but forgiveness will heal. Then let children forgive their parents. Many parents have not been all they should have been, but despite all they have failed to be, let us forgive and set them free. Then let bosses forgive their employees, and let employees forgive their bosses. Let church members forgive one another, and let politicians forgive one another. Let pastors forgive one another, and let students forgive one another. Let the spirit of forgiveness bring healing to our tongues and cause us to forever cease to speak ill of one another.

Endnote

1. R.T. Kendall, *Total Forgiveness* (Lake Mary, FL: Charisma House, 2002), xii-xiii.

Chapter 10

How to Have a Good Life

For he that will love life, and see good days, let
him refrain his tongue from evil, and his lips
that they speak no guile (1 Peter 3:10).

THERE IS MUCH more that could be said about this most important matter of gossip and evil reporting, but suffice it to say that
the apostle Peter has spoken to us the end of the matter. In the
Book of First Peter, he admonished his fellow saints not to return
evil for evil, or railing (verbal assault) for railing (see 1 Pet. 3:9).
He reminds them of the character God expects from us as saints.
Then, in chapter 3 verse 10, he offers the saints what I call the
key to having a good life. The apostle Peter says that this key
is to *"refrain* [one's] *tongue from evil, and* [one's] *lips that they
speak no guile."* Wow! It's just that simple. If God were to tell us
directly that He was going to give us the key to having a good
life and seeing good days, we would expect that God would give
us a manual on life—or at least a few prophetic visions. Yet,

the revelation Peter shares with us, as God's instruction on how to have a good life, is so simple that a child could not err. He simply says, in essence, "Watch your mouth!"

Gossip, slander, judging, evil reporting, and all other forms of unholy talk are a sure way to have a sad life, have few friendships, and lose your inheritance. I have met many people who are given to gossip, and all of them seem to live beleaguered and unfulfilled lives. They can be living in the largest house in the neighborhood, but their lives and the enjoyment of their blessings can be zapped away by the fact that they talk negatively about other people. Because of incontinent speech, for many people, happiness is illusive. On the other hand, if we can love those we have formerly spoken evil of, we will inherit from God a joy that is unspeakable and full of glory. If we want to live the good life, it is not that complicated to do; we just have to change our conversation. As my grandmother used to say, "Watch your mouth!"

A Prophetic Word

And I heard a loud voice saying in heaven, "Now is come salvation, and strength, and the kingdom of our God, and the power of His Christ: for the accuser of our brethren is cast down, which accused them before God day and night" (Revelation 12:10).

In conclusion, I want to return to the Scripture that started us on our journey. In Revelation 12:10, satan is revealed as the accuser of the brethren. We have gone through several chapters expounding upon this reality. There is yet another very powerful revelation in this verse that has application to the Church today. The above verse says, *"...Now is come salvation, and strength, and the kingdom of our God, and the power of His Christ: for the accuser of our brethren is cast down...."* I have read this verse many times, but one day I was reading it and the Holy Spirit spoke to me and said, "The hindrance to the Kingdom of God being ushered in on earth is the presence of the accuser within the Body of Christ. Unless and until the accuser is cast down, you will be ineffective at ushering in the Kingdom of God." The verse says, *"Now is come...."* This means that as soon as the accuser is cast out, the Kingdom of God will be ushered in. As long as there is room for the accuser among the saints, the Kingdom we all await will be hindered. It is time for the saints to bind and loose. As we bind the accuser spirit and renounce gossip, the Kingdom of God will become evident among us and the power of God will be manifested.

Chapter 11

Meditation: For Victory Over Gossip

MEDITATION ON GOD'S Word is a powerful tool we can use to overcome any personal weakness. God told Joshua to meditate on His Word day and night in order to be successful (see Josh. 1:8). Meditation will assist both the individual who has had to face the shame of being gossiped about and the person who is trying to overcome the tendency to gossip. The Scriptures in this chapter have been chosen for the purpose of meditation. To overcome gossip, we must re-program our minds by thinking and speaking in accordance with the Word of God.

Read each of the Scriptures below. Focus on what it is saying about gossip, our daily conversation, and how God feels about negative speech. Then meditate upon it, and ask God to help you to implement its wisdom into your daily life. Those who have been the subject of gossip should focus on how many biblical characters have had to deal with the challenge of being gossiped about, people's opinions about them, and personal sin. Then ask God to help you to walk in victory over the negative things that have been said about you. I have provided a "Focus" section before each Scripture. The Focus section will help you to get the major points. Let God speak to your heart as you read each Scripture. Then use these and other Scriptures as daily confessions for a life of victory over gossip.

Scripture for Meditation

Focus: In the Bible, *dog* is an idiom for Gentile people. In the following two Scriptures, God is showing us that when He redeemed the Israelites from Egypt, they became His chosen people. He set them apart as an example to the unsaved. It is God's goal and will that the unsaved would not be able to speak one bad word against the saved, as a witness that they have been redeemed.

> *But against the children of Israel shall not a dog move his tongue, against man or beast: that ye may know how that the Lord doth put a difference between the Egyptians and Israel* (Exodus 11:7).

> *And all the people returned to the camp to Joshua at Makkedah in peace: and none moved his tongue against any of the children of Israel* (Joshua 10:21).

Focus: Here is a picture of a gossiping community—people who are intent on diminishing others with their mouths. They are double-hearted and disloyal. They know their mouths are out of control, but they despise the idea of God ruling over their tongues.

They speak vanity everyone with his neighbor: with flattering lips and a double heart do they speak. The Lord shall cut off all flattering lips, and the tongue that speaketh proud things. Who have said, "With our tongue will we prevail; our lips are our own: who is lord over us?" (Psalm 12:2-4)

Focus: Often when they hear a negative report about others, people of corrupt character will add false testimony to what has already been said. Often those who are gossiped about have to deal with people exploiting them by telling the negative parts of their story. But they also have to deal with the exaggerations and falsehoods of people who are just cruel and heartless.

Deliver me not over unto the will of mine enemies: for false witnesses are risen up against me, and such as breathe out cruelty (Psalm 27:12).

Focus: This next psalm is for those who have been gossiped about. Maybe some personal choice or failure has left you the subject of the talk of many. Don't give up, and don't let your heart fail. God uses imperfect people. In the text below, David acknowledges his "iniquity" to be the source of the gossip. Even though he is not innocent, he still grabs hold of the mercy of God. People who knew of his faults separated themselves from him. Both his friends and his enemies refused to own him. But David held to God and to His love for him. You too need to hold to God's unchanging hand. The strife of tongues is when a person is being belittled, embarrassed, or debased by a group of people. David's testimony was that God hid him in His pavilion away from the scourge of the tongue.

For my life is spent with grief, and my years with sighing: my strength faileth because of mine iniquity, and my bones are consumed. I was a reproach among all mine enemies, but especially among neighbors, and a fear to mine acquaintances: they that did see me without fled from me. I am forgotten as a dead man out of mind: I am like a broken vessel. For I have heard the slander of many: fear was on every side: while they took counsel together against me, they devised to take away my life...Let the lying lips be put to silence; which speak grievous things proudly and contemptuously against the righteous. Oh how great is Thy goodness, which Thou hast laid up for them that fear Thee: which Thou hast wrought for them that trust in Thee before the sons of men. Thou shalt hide them in the secret of Thy presence from the pride of man; Thou shalt keep them secretly in a pavilion from the strife of tongues...Be of good courage, and He shall strengthen your heart, all ye that hope in the Lord (Psalm 31:10-13,18-20,24).

Focus: Gossip brings people social hurt. It hurts their name, their reputation, and their families. Some people who are zealous for gossip will even testify that they have seen or heard things that they did not. We must learn to speak things that will bring peace and not confusion and shame. But no matter what is said about you, make sure you govern your conversation in a righteous way. Let no man or woman pull you down into unrighteous retaliation.

False witnesses did rise up; they laid to my charge things that I knew not...With hypocritical mockers in feasts, they gnash upon me with their teeth...For they speak not peace: but they devise matters against them that are quiet in the land. Yea they opened their mouth wide against me, and said, "Aha, aha, our eye hath seen it"...Let them be ashamed and brought to confusion together that rejoice at my hurt: let them be clothed with shame and dishonor that magnify themselves against me...And my tongue shall speak of Thy righteousness and of Thy praise all the day long (Psalm 35:11,16,20-21,26,28).

Focus: Many believers give their mouths to evil. Some have even turned their tongues on their own brothers and sisters. If you are a believer who associates with a slanderer, and you never say anything confronting that person's toxic tongue, then you are just as much guilty as the one who is doing the talking.

Thou givest thy mouth to evil, and thy tongue frame deceit. Thou sittest and speakest against thy brother; thou slanderest thine own mother's son. These things hast thou done, and I kept silence; thou thoughtest that I was altogether such an one as thyself: but I will reprove thee, and set them in order before thine eyes...Whoso offereth praise glorifieth Me: and to him that ordereth his conversation aright will I shew the salvation of God (Psalm 50:19-21,23).

Focus: Some people's problem is that their flesh loves to gossip. They would rather see someone pulled down by talk than built up in faith.

Thy tongue deviseth mischief; like a mighty razor, working deceitfully. Thou loveth evil more than good;

and lying rather than to speak righteousness, Selah. Thou lovest devouring words, O deceitful tongue. God shall likewise destroy thee forever, He shall take thee away, and pluck thee out of thy dwelling place, and root thee out of the land of the living. Selah" (Psalm 52:2-5).

Focus: Satan is the accuser of the brethren, and it is his voice that is always going forth to condemn us before God and people. It is that voice that is always testifying that you did this or that, casting iniquity on you. There is nothing more discouraging than when a fellow saint is being used by the accuser to bad-mouth you. But God is still God.

Give ear to my prayer, O God; and hide not Thyself from my supplication. Attend unto me, and hear me: I mourn in my complaint, and make a noise; because of the voice of the enemy, because of the oppression of the wicked: for they cast iniquity upon me, and in wrath they hate me...For it was not an enemy that reproached me, then I could have borne it: neither was it he that hated me that did magnify himself against me; then I would have hid myself from him. But it was thou, a man mine equal, my guide, and mine acquaintance. We took sweet counsel together, and walked into the house of God in company...God shall hear, and afflict them, even He that abideth of old. Selah. Because they have no changes, therefore they fear not God (Psalm 55:1-3, 12-14, 19).

Focus: To slander someone means to speak words that will damage a person's character or reputation. It is pride that makes one person feel justified in badmouthing another.

Whoso privily slandereth his neighbor, him will I cut off: him that hath a high look and a proud heart will I not suffer (Psalm 101:5).

Focus: Words are powerful. They are trafficked through the spirit realm and they affect our lives. When people speak evil of you, they are placing weights on you in the spirit realm. There is a literal fight in your life to keep the spirit realm clear of oppressive and negative conversation about you. You need God's help in this fight.

Hold not Thy peace, O God of my praise; for the mouth of the wicked and the mouth of the deceitful are open against me: they have spoken against me with a lying tongue. They compassed me about also with words of hatred; and fought against me without a cause (Psalm 109:1-3).

Focus: If you have been the subject of gossip, you need to know that you can call upon the Lord about the matter. A deceitful tongue is a misleading tongue. It represents someone who makes people think the worst of you.

In my distress I cried unto the Lord, and He heard me. Deliver my soul, O Lord, from lying lips, and from a deceitful tongue (Psalm 120:1-2).

Focus: According to Proverbs 6, three of the six things God hates are *"a lying tongue,"* *"a false witness that speaketh lies,"* and *"he that soweth discord among brethren."* These three, of the six things God hates, have to do with your mouth.

These six things doth the Lord hate: yea seven are an abomination unto Him: a proud look, a lying tongue, and hands that shed innocent blood, an heart that deviseth wicked imaginations, feet that be swift to run to mischief, a false witness that speaketh lies, and he that soweth discord among the brethren (Proverbs 6:16-19).

Focus: You cannot be a good neighbor when you are inclined to gossip. God is concerned about your city and its welfare. Your conversation has a lot to do with that.

A hypocrite with his mouth destroyeth his neighbor... When it goeth well with the righteous, the city rejoiceth: and when the wicked perish, there is shouting. By the blessing of the upright the city is exalted: but it is overthrown by the mouth of the wicked. He that is void of wisdom despiseth his neighbor: but a man of understanding holdeth his peace. A talebearer revealeth secrets: but he that is of a faithful spirit concealeth the matter (Proverbs 11:9-13).

Focus: Ask God to deliver you from lying. Ask Him to help you to speak the truth always.

Lying lips are abomination to the Lord: but they that deal truly are His delight (Proverbs 12:22).

Focus: I know of people who lost jobs, friends, money, and even their lives because they didn't know how to keep their mouth closed.

He that keepeth his mouth keepeth his life: but he that openeth his mouth wide his lips shall have destruction (Proverbs 13:3).

Focus: The people who are over you in your job or in your life will take notice of how you talk. Your conversation is directly related to your promotion in life.

Righteous lips are the delight of kings; and they love him that speaketh right (Proverbs 16:13).

Focus: We should do unto others as we would have them do unto us. If we would not want others to tell things about us, we should do the same for them.

Excellent speech becometh not a fool: much less do lying lips a prince...He that covereth a transgression seeketh love; but he that repeateth a matter separateth friends (Proverbs 17:7,9).

Focus: Many people have been hurt by gossip. When you hear something bad about others, you should be emotionally disciplined enough to allow them to explain themselves before you render a judgment. What you are saying out of your mouth about your life will cause you to have success or failure.

The words of a talebearer are as wounds, and they go down into the innermost parts...He that answereth a matter before he heareth it, it is folly and shame unto him...A man's belly shall be satisfied with the fruit of his mouth; and with the increase of his lips shall he be filled. Death and life are in the power of the tongue:

and they that love it shall eat the fruit thereof (Proverbs 18:8,13,20-21).

Focus: In many places in Scripture, God says He hates when people give a false witness. We should be extra careful to be sure that the things we say about other people are true.

A false witness shall not be unpunished, and he that speaketh lies shall not escape (Proverbs 19:5).

Focus: Some people, so seemingly innocent, love to tell everything they know. "Did you hear this...?" or "Did you hear that...?" is how they talk. Although they seem innocent, their words are evil nonetheless.

He that goeth about as a talebearer revealeth secrets: therefore meddle not with him that flattereth with his lips (Proverbs 20:19).

Focus: Some people are quick to argue. Others are quick to "put someone in their place." But this type of disposition leads to strife. Still other people will retell something they heard before they confirm whether or not it is true. We all have heard someone angrily confronted with, "I heard you have been talking about me!"

Go not forth hastily to strive, lest thou know not what to do in the end thereof, when thy neighbor hath put thee to shame. Debate thy cause with thy neighbor himself; discover not a secret to another (Proverbs 25:8-9).

Focus: Many arguments and strife would die if someone would just stop talking.

Where no wood is, there the fire goeth out: so where there is no talebearer, the strife ceaseth. As coals are to burning coals, and wood to fire; so is a contentious man to kindle strife. The words of a talebearer are as wounds, and they go down into the innermost parts of the belly. Burning lips and a wicked heart are like a pot potsherd covered with silver dross. He that dissembleth with his lips and layeth up deceit within him. When he speaketh fair, believe him not: for there are seven abominations in his heart (Proverbs 26:20-25).

Focus: The *remnant* in Scripture refers to those who are left after God's judgment. We should consider that these are the types of people God is pleased with.

The remnant of Israel shall not do iniquity, nor speak lies; neither shall a deceitful tongue be found in their mouth: for they shall feed and lie down, and none shall make them afraid (Zephaniah 3:13).

Focus: When you gossip, you support the enemy's opposition to the preaching of the Gospel.

And it came to pass in Iconium, that they went both [Paul and Barnabas] together into the synagogue of the Jews, and so spake, that a great multitude both of the Jews and also of the Greeks believed. But the unbelieving Jews stirred up the Gentiles, and made their minds evil affected against the brethren (Acts 14:1-2).

Focus: Unrighteous speech grieves the Holy Spirit.

Let no corrupt communication proceed out of your mouth, but that which is good to the use of edifying, that it may minister grace unto the hearers. And grieve not the Holy Spirit of God, whereby ye are sealed unto the day of redemption. Let all bitterness, and wrath, and anger, and clamor, and evil speaking [gossip] be put away from you, with all malice (Ephesians 4:29-31).

Focus: We put a bridle on a horse to control it. So we must have a bridle on our own tongues. Our hearts listen to our mouths and not to our religious acts. Therefore, even if people are doing religious service, their hearts will invariably follow their mouths.

If any man among you seem to be religious, and bridleth not his tongue, but deceiveth his own heart, this man's religion is in vain (James 1:26).

Focus: The apostle John was vehemently opposed and talked about by people who were members of the church.

Wherefore, if I come, I will remember his deeds which he doeth, talking against us with malicious words: and not content therewith, neither does he himself receive the brethren, and forbiddeth them that would, and casteth them out of the church (3 John 10).

Meditate on these things!

About Mark D. Michael

MARK D. MICHAEL is the pastor of the New Life Christian Center in Union Springs, Alabama. He is a gifted pastor and teacher who is sought after for his gift of revelation knowledge of the Scriptures.

Pastor Michael is the author of three books:

Overcoming Gossip

Don't Give It Another Thought

Righteousness: God's Gift to You!

To contact Pastor Michael, please e-mail him at:
Pastormdmichael@yahoo.com

IN THE RIGHT HANDS, THIS BOOK WILL CHANGE LIVES!

Most of the people who need this message will not be looking for this book. To change their lives, you need to put a copy of this book in their hands.

> *But others (seeds) fell into good ground, and brought forth fruit, some a hundred-fold, some sixty-fold, some thirty-fold* (Matthew 13:8).

Our ministry is constantly seeking methods to find the good ground, the people who need this anointed message to change their lives. Will you help us reach these people?

> *Remember this—a farmer who plants only a few seeds will get a small crop. But the one who plants generously will get a generous crop* (2 Corinthians 9:6).

EXTEND THIS MINISTRY BY SOWING
3 BOOKS, 5 BOOKS, 10 BOOKS, OR MORE TODAY,
AND BECOME A LIFE CHANGER!

Thank you,

Don Nori Sr., Founder
Destiny Image
Since 1982